First Workshop on Resources for African Indigenous Languages (RAIL 2020)

Marseille, France
11-16 May 2020

Editors:

Rooweither Mabuya
Phathutshedzo Ramukhadi
Mmasibidi Setaka
Valencia Wagner
Menno van Zaanen

ISBN: 978-1-7138-1274-6

Printed from e-media with permission by:

Curran Associates, Inc.
57 Morehouse Lane
Red Hook, NY 12571

CURRAN ASSOCIATES INC. proceedings.com

Some format issues inherent in the e-media version may also appear in this print version.

Association for Computational Linguistics
209 N. Eighth Street
Stroudsburg, Pennsylvania 18360

Phone: 1-570-476-8006
Fax: 1-570-476-0860

acl@aclweb.org

Additional copies of this publication are available from:

Curran Associates, Inc.
57 Morehouse Lane
Red Hook, NY 12571 USA
Phone: 845-758-0400
Fax: 845-758-2633
Email: curran@proceedings.com
Web: www.proceedings.com

LREC 2020 Workshop
Language Resources and Evaluation Conference
11–16 May 2020

First workshop on
Resources for African Indigenous Languages
(RAIL)

PROCEEDINGS

Editors:

Rooweither Mabuya, Phathutshedzo Ramukhadi, Mmasibidi Setaka, Valencia Wagner, Menno van Zaanen

Proceedings of the LREC 2020 first workshop on Resources for African Indigenous Languages (RAIL)

Edited by:
Rooweither Mabuya, Phathutshedzo Ramukhadi, Mmasibidi Setaka, Valencia Wagner, and Menno van Zaanen

For more information:
European Language Resources Association (ELRA)
9 rue des Cordelières
75013, Paris
France
http://www.elra.info
Email: lrec@elda.org

Introduction

Africa is a multilingual continent with an estimation of 1500 to 2000 indigenous languages. Many of these languages currently have no or very limited language resources available, and are often structurally quite different from more well-resourced languages, therefore requiring the development and use of specialized techniques.

The Resources for African Indigenous Languages (RAIL) workshop is an interdisciplinary platform for researchers working on resources (data collections, tools, etc.) specifically targeted towards African indigenous languages to provide an overview of the current state-of-the-art and emphasize the availability of African indigenous language resources, including both data and tools.

With the UNESCO-supported International Year of Indigenous Languages, there is currently much interest in indigenous languages. The Permanent Forum on Indigenous Issues mentioned that "40 percent of the estimated 6,700 languages spoken around the world were in danger of disappearing" and the "languages represent complex systems of knowledge and communication and should be recognized as a strategic national resource for development, peace building and reconciliation." As such, the workshop falls within one of the hot topic areas of this year's conference: "Less Resourced and Endangered Languages".

In total, 24, in general, very high quality submissions were received. Out of these 9 submissions were selected using double blind review for presentation in the workshop. Unfortunately, due to the Covid-19 pandemic, the physical workshop had to be cancelled, however, it is replaced by a virtual workshop.

The topics on which the call for papers was issued are the following:

- Computational linguistics for African indigenous languages
- Descriptions of corpora or other data sets of African indigenous languages
- Building resources for (under resourced) African indigenous languages
- Developing and using African indigenous languages in the digital age
- Effectiveness of digital technologies for the development of African indigenous languages
- Revealing unknown or unpublished existing resources for African indigenous languages
- Developing desired resources for African indigenous languages
- Improving quality, availability and accessibility of African indigenous language resources

The goals for the workshop are:

- to bring together researchers who are interested in showcasing their research and thereby boosting the field of African indigenous languages,
- to create the conditions for the emergence of a scientific community of practice that focuses on data, as well as tools, specifically designed for or applied to indigenous languages found in Africa,
- to create conversations between academics and researchers in different fields such as African indigenous languages, computational linguistics, sociolinguistics and language technology, and
- to provide an opportunity for the African indigenous languages community to identify, describe and share their Language Resources.

Organizers:

Rooweither Mabuya
Phathutshedzo Ramukhadi
Mmasibidi Setaka
Valencia Wagner
Menno van Zaanen
South African centre for Digital Language Resources (SADiLaR), South Africa

Program Committee:

Richard Ajah, University of Uyo, Nigeria
Ayodele James Akinola, Chrisland University, Nigeria
Felix Ameka, Leiden University, the Netherlands
Sonja Bosch, University of South Africa, South Africa
Ibrahima Cissé, University of Humanities, Mali
Roald Eiselen, Eiselen software consulting, South Africa
Tanja Gaustad, Centre for Text Technology, South Africa
Elias Malete, University of the Free State, South Africa
Dimakatso Mathe, South African centre for Digital Language Resources, South Africa
Elias Mathipa, University of South Africa, South Africa
Fekede Menuta, Hawassa University, Ethiopia
Innocentia Mhlambi, Wits University, South Africa
Emmanuel Ngue Um, University of Yaoundé I, Cameroon
Guy de Pauw, Antwerp University and Textgain, Belgium
Sara Petrollino, Leiden University, the Netherlands
Pule Phindane, Central University of Technology, South Africa
Danie Prinsloo, University of Pretoria, South Africa
Martin Puttkammer, Centre for Text Technology, South Africa
Justus Roux, Stellenbosch University, South Africa
Msindisi Sam, Rhodes University, South Africa
Gilles-Maurice de Schryver, Ghent University, Belgium
Lorraine Shabangu, Bangula Lingo Centre, South Africa
Elsabé Taljard, University of Pretoria, South Africa

Table of Contents

Conference Program

9:00–9:10 ***Opening/Introduction***

09:10–09:30 *Endangered African Languages Featured in a Digital Collection: The Case of the Khomani San, Hugh Brody Collection*
Kerry Jones and Sanjin Muftic

09:30–09:50 *Usability and Accessibility of Bantu Language Dictionaries in the Digital Age: Mobile Access in an Open Environment*
Thomas Eckart, Sonja Bosch, Uwe Quasthoff, Erik Körner, Dirk Goldhahn and Simon Kaleschke

09:50–10:10 *Investigating an Approach for Low Resource Language Dataset Creation, Curation and Classification: Setswana and Sepedi*
Vukosi Marivate, Tshephisho Sefara and Abiodun Modupe

10:10–10:30 *Complex Setswana Parts of Speech Tagging*
Gabofetswe Malema, Boago Okgetheng, Bopaki Tebalo, Moffat Motlhanka and Goaletsa Rammidi

10:30–10:50 *Comparing Neural Network Parsers for a Less-resourced and Morphologically-rich Language: Amharic Dependency Parser*
Binyam Ephrem Seyoum, Yusuke Miyao and Baye Yimam Mekonnen

10:50–11:10 *Mobilizing Metadata: Open Data Kit (ODK) for Language Resource Development in East Africa*
Richard Griscom

11:10–11:40 ***Coffee break***

11:40–12:00 *A Computational Grammar of Ga*
Lars Hellan

12:00–12:20 *Navigating Challenges of Multilingual Resource Development for Under-Resourced Languages: The Case of the African Wordnet Project*
Marissa Griesel and Sonja Bosch

12:20–12:40 *Building Collaboration-based Resources in Endowed African Languages: Case of NTeALan Dictionaries Platform*
Elvis Mboning Tchiaze, Jean Marc Bassahak, Daniel Baleba, Ornella Wandji and Jules Assoumou

12:40–13:00 ***Closing***

Proceedings of the First workshop on Resources for African Indigenous Languages (RAIL), pages 1–8
Language Resources and Evaluation Conference (LREC 2020), Marseille, 11–16 May 2020

Endangered African Languages Featured in a Digital Collection: The Case of the ǂKhomani San | Hugh Brody Collection

Kerry Jones, Sanjin Muftic
Director, African Tongue, Linguistics Consultancy, Cape Town, South Africa
Postdoctoral Research Fellow, English Language and Linguistics, Rhodes University, Makhanda, South Africa
Research Associate, Department of General Linguistics, Stellenbosch University, Stellenbosch, South Africa;
Digital Scholarship Specialist, Digital Library Services, University of Cape Town, South Africa
jonesleekerry@gmail.com, sanjin.muftic@uct.ac.za

Abstract

The ǂKhomani San | Hugh Brody Collection features the voices and history of indigenous hunter gatherer descendants in three endangered languages namely, N|uu, Kora and Khoekhoe as well as a regional dialect of Afrikaans. A large component of this collection is audio-visual (legacy media) recordings of interviews conducted with members of the community by Hugh Brody and his colleagues between 1997 and 2012, referring as far back as the 1800s. The Digital Library Services team at the University of Cape Town aim to showcase the collection digitally on the UCT-wide Digital Collections platform, Ibali which runs on Omeka-S. In this paper we highlight the importance of such a collection in the context of South Africa, and the ethical steps that were taken to ensure the respect of the ǂKhomani San as their stories get uploaded onto a repository and become accessible to all. We will also feature some of the completed collection on Ibali and guide the reader through the organisation of the collection on the Omeka-S backend. Finally, we will outline our development process, from digitisation to repository publishing as well as present some of the challenges in data clean-up, the curation of legacy media, multi-lingual support, and site organisation.

Keywords: endangered African languages, N|uu, Kora, Khoekhoe, digital curation, online showcasing, heritage knowledge, ethics of repositories

1. Introduction

Language endangerment and language loss is a worldwide phenomenon and the African context is no exception to this loss of linguistic diversity. As a result, the scramble to identify, document and preserve indigenous languages using digital technology has gained traction. Despite vast research in the field of language vitality, "relatively little is known about Africa's endangered languages" (Kandybowicz & Torrence, 2017). In Southern Africa, identification and documentation of endangered languages in collaboration with indigenous communities has only fairly recently begun. Records of such efforts are dispersed in various locations around the world. In the instance of the ǂKhomani San | Hugh Brody Collection, South Africa is fortunate to have secured the return of this valuable collection. Upon its return, we were then faced with the challenge of making the contents of the collection freely available and not reserved for the select few.

The potential solution to this problem was to host the collection on a digital platform. The Digital Library Services (DLS) at the University of Cape Town (UCT) suggested the use of their Digital Collections platform, Ibali, which runs on Omeka-S and could accommodate open access. The digital curation process required a number of different steps, from setting up a workflow, to organising the collection data within particular schemas. Once the data was organised within the predetermined schemas, the data could then be hosted on the platform in a structured manner. In this paper we discuss the different phases of collection development with a particular focus on the processes undertaken to publish the collection through an institutional repository. Throughout these processes we encountered many questions, challenges, debates and potential solutions revolving around how to best digitally curate this collection in an ethical and user-friendly way. This collection serves as an important example of representing indigenous knowledge via a digital platform. Furthermore, it describes a methodology to decolonise the archive while maintaining international standards.

By curating an output that is accessible to speakers of endangered languages, the South African public and academics, we created a more inclusive online environment for understanding our historical and contemporary South African context. It must however be noted that lack of access to a reliable internet connection and electricity does preclude many South Africans from being able to readily access online content. Households in South Africa with the least access to communication media are from the Northern Cape (10.3%), which is also the province where the majority of N|uu, Kora and Khoekhoe speakers live (Statistics South Africa, 2018, 36). Such challenges are overcome through access to resources via state and privately funded libraries and computer centres.

2. Ethical Considerations and Community Collaboration

The choice to house and curate the collection in South Africa was an ethical decision made by Hugh Brody in collaboration with Open Channels, a charity organisation based in the United Kingdom, the ǂKhomani San Community and the South African San Institute (SASI), a local non-government organisation. By physically hosting the collection locally, this makes its contents more accessible to South Africans as opposed to having the collection hosted at an overseas institution. International travel is financially out of reach to the majority of the South African population, most especially minority groups such as the descendants of the ǂKhomani San. The collaboration between all interested parties and UCT was expressed in a Gift Agreement outlining the contents of the collection. As part of this agreement, UCT committed to processing, cataloguing and ensuring the collection was freely accessible. This collaboration and contractual agreement became the launching pad for future collaborations and work to come.

3. Linguistic Context of the Featured Languages in South Africa

In Southern Africa there are three language families that were previously grouped together and known as Khoesan languages (Heine & Honken, 2010). Today, Khoesan languages are more accurately described as Ju, Khoe and Tuu languages which is in accordance with the Comparative Method in linguistics (Güldemann, 2008, 123). All three of these language families are endangered and are associated with traditional hunter gatherers and pastoralists, also known as San and Khoe respectively. At the time of their initial documentation there were approximately 35 languages known to science from the Ju, Khoe and Tuu language families (Voβen, 2013). Since then, several of these languages have gone extinct, with only 13 remaining, of which 6 are spoken in South Africa (Jones, 2019).

Ju, Khoe and Tuu languages and their click sounds are a hallmark of Southern African linguistic and cultural heritage. Yet efforts made in research, development and preservation of Khoe and San heritage often falls short when it comes to meaningful community collaboration and accessibility to the content produced. Accountability and accessibility to historical and contemporary research pertaining to Khoe and San peoples is paramount to equity and democratisation of knowledge dissemination in Southern Africa. Khoe and San peoples have a documented history fraught with conflict, dispossession, and identity and language loss resulting in today's context as being minority marginalised groups scattered across Southern Africa.

The ǂKhomani San | Hugh Brody Collection documents the stories of the ǂKhomani people over the last 100 years entailing detailed accounts of linguistic and cultural genocide. Through a process of a cultural audit lead by Nigel Crawhall in collaboration with the United Nations Educational, Scientific and Cultural Organization (UNESCO) and the SASI (Crawhall, 2001) 24 remaining speakers of N|uu made themselves known. N|uu was previously thought to be extinct and belongs to the Tuu or more specifically the !Ui-Taa language family, our most fragile of the three families. Today, only three mother tongue speakers of N|uu remain and it is therefore classified as a severely endangered language.

Upon further engagement with community members of the ǂKhomani San it was revealed that some could speak Kora also known as !Ora as a second language. Recordings and transcriptions of such examples can be found in the ǂKhomani San | Hugh Brody Collection. Today Kora is considered moribund (du Plessis, 2018). It was also evident that speakers of N|uu had undergone language shifts to Afrikaans and Khoekhoe. Afrikaans is the historically dominant language during the apartheid era in South Africa and Namibia. Whereas, Khoekhoe also known as Khoekhoegowab, is the lingua franca of the Kalahari with approximately only 2000 speakers remaining in South Africa (Witzlack-Makarevich, 2006, 12).

The utilisation of data from the ǂKhomani San | Hugh Brody Collection was instrumental in several successful land claims in the Northern Cape, South Africa. It is therefore not only a historical and linguistic record of South African history but a unique collection of evidence that resulted in restitution for the ǂKhomani San.

4. Samples from the Collection

What is unique about the ǂKhomani San | Hugh Brody Collection is that it is based in southern Africa and was actively created with the ǂKhomani San community members and researchers not only during the creation of the data but the processing of it too. The ǂKhomani San | Hugh Brody Collection comprises mainly of audio-visual (legacy media) recordings of interviews conducted with members of the community by Hugh Brody and his team between 1997 and 2012. The initial project was motivated by the plight of the community who had been dispossessed from their ancestral land. Through genealogical mapping and detailed interviews, the team was able to support a successful land claim on behalf of the community in 1999, when President Mbeki personally visited to return the land to its rightful owners. Subsequent successful land claims in the area were to follow. Fieldwork continued until 2012, after which the collection was deposited in trust to UCT at Special Collections, UCT Libraries in 2013 (BVF-41 Project Plan). The collection consists of various data types such as transcripts, videos, audio clips, maps and images. Below are some examples of transcript files, photographs and maps that illustrate this highly collaborative data production process.

4.1 Transcript files

The transcript files in the collection are based on over 128 hours of film footage of which more than 30 hours include speech that has been transcribed to date. The transcriptions are verbatim, and colour coded in either N|uu (green), Kora (orange), Khoekhoe (red) or Afrikaans (blue) and translated into English (black), including timing notations. The transcript files are colour coded to assist the reader in easily identifying the different languages transcribed and translated in each transcript file. The process of creating the transcript files was highly collaborative including linguists specialising in each of the languages found in the collection and hands-on verification with mother tongue speakers throughout the transcription and translation process. The challenge with working with a newly developed orthography for N|uu in the field of linguistics, resulted in the development of a multilingual dictionary featuring N|uu with accompanying translations into Afrikaans, Khoekhoe and English for over 1400 lexical entries (Sands et al., 2006).

Table 1 is an example from transcript 1998_01-01 as spoken by Katriena |Una Kassie Rooi where she mixes Afrikaans and N|uu when explaining who she is and where she comes from. For the purposes of a black and white publication the Afrikaans in the transcription column is in roman text and the N|uu in italics.

Time code: 00:00:05	
English translation	Transcription
|Una: Yes, I am now a Bushman. I am a pure Bushman. My father was a Bushman. My mother was a Bushman. My father's father was a Bushman. That is the reason that I am a Bushman. I am |Una. My father was ǂHan. My grandfather was old Hans Kassie. My father was Tities Kassie. He was old Hans Kassie's child. I am now |Una who is the daughter of old Tities Kassie.	|Una: Ja, *ng ke* nou n *Saasi.* Ek is n regte *Saasi. Ng ainki ke n Saasi. Ng xainki a ng Saasi. Ng ainki ke ng Saasi. Ke a gao ke ng Saasi. Ng ke ng |Una. Ng ainki a n ǂHan. Ng* oupa *ng* ou Hans Kassie. Dis nou my pa is Tities Kassie. Dis ou Hans Kassie se kind. Ek is nou *|Una*, wat ou Tities Kassie se dogter.

Table 1: Excerpt from transcript file 1998_01-01 in Afrikaans and N|uu translated into English

Table 2 is an example from the transcript 2001_01-04 as spoken by Anna Swarts as she tells a traditional story in Khoekhoe about the Jackal and the Hyena. She tells of a time before there was order in the universe and animals were humans.

Time code: 00:00:11	
English translation	Transcription
Anna: Thanks, my brother. My brother, it was like this. When the jackal and the hyena were human beings… the jackal was actually the clever one. Then he said: "Oh, we are dying of hunger. So, what should we do?" The Hyena responded: "Do like this, do like this. You are the man, isn't it? So you should make a plan." Then the jackal went back and laid down in the road.	Anna: Aio ti !gâ. Ti !gâ, nēti i ge ge ī i. ǁNā, kō, ǂhīras tsi |girab tsîra ge khoe io, os ge... |Girab ge hūka ge gā-aisa ge ūhâ i. Ob ge ǁîba "Ēse, !âs xam ta ǁō. Om nî mati dī?" (ǂHīras:...) Nē, nēti dī, nēti dī re, sats kom a aoreo, xuige satsa |awe-e dī re." Ob ge |giriba oa tsi ge daob !nâ sī ge ǁgoe.

Table 2: Excerpt from transcript file 2001_01-04, traditional folklore told in Khoekhoe and translated into English

4.2 Photographs

Photographs from the collection range from the early 1900s to 1999. Those from the beginning of the 20th century were selected by researchers in the 1990s from UCT's archives, copied and taken along to the southern Kalahari. When interviewing community members, researchers would show the old photographs from UCT and explain that they were trying to learn more about the original people from the area. During this process, Elsie Vaalbooi recognised a photograph of herself (Figure 1) and another of her mother (Figure 2) taken circa 1911. This was the first time she had seen these photographs since they were taken. Elsie was one of the last speakers of N|uu and today her son, Petrus Vaalbooi (Figure 3), is the traditional leader of the ǂKhomani San.

The collection of photographs encompasses many themes such as: individual and family portraits; indigenous fauna and flora used by the ǂKhomani San; culturally or historically important places; language work (as seen in Figure 4); and physical evidence of occupation in the Kalahari Transfrontier Park by the ǂKhomani San before their eviction.

Figure 1 & 2: Photograph of Elsie Vaalbooi (standing) and her mother Marie ||Qoesi (sitting) circa 1911.

Figure 3: Photograph of Elsie Vaalbooi and her son Petrus Vaalbooi taken shortly before Elsie died in 1997.

Figure 4: Linguist Nigel Crawhall (sunglasses around his neck), working with Dawid Kruiper (hand pointing over page) and family on trilingual wordlists

4.3 Maps

Several detailed maps were created in collaboration with community members, linguists and cartographers to visually represent the ǂKhomani San genealogy and movements of different family members over time. The GIS data collected provided the necessary input to produce accurate maps representing place names in Khoekhoe, Afrikaans and English as seen in Figure 5. The variety of Afrikaans spoken by the ǂKhomani San community members is unique to the area and provided great insight into the original place names of the southern Kalahari.

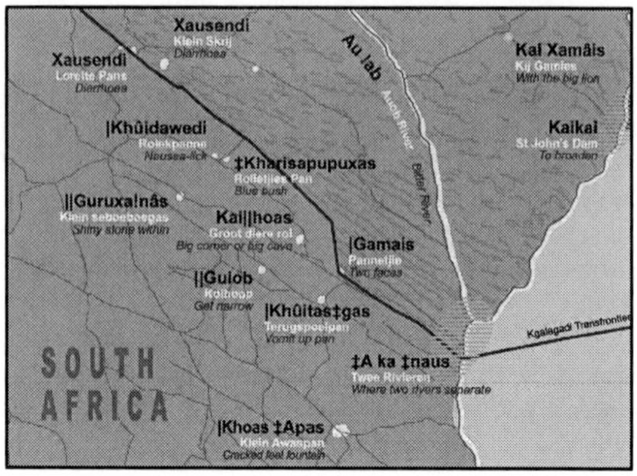

Figure 5: Map of traditional place names in Khoekhoe, Afrikaans and English within and surrounding the Kgalagadi Transfrontier Park

5. Organisation of the Collection on the Omeka-S Backend

The collection has gone through several phases of development, including the ongoing addition of detailed transcripts of the legacy media by specialist linguistics company African Tongue (Director, Kerry Jones). Elements of the collection were previously published online through an Islandora (Fedora Commons) website which provided basic archival description of selected media. However, the website did not provide a way of navigating the collection beyond those descriptions and therefore had to be revised. Consequently, the decision was made to publish the collection through UCT's institution wide collection repository, Ibali, powered by Omeka-S.

The online exhibition tool Omeka-S, in conjunction with the IIIF server, is widely used internationally by university libraries, and the majority of the Galleries, Libraries, Archives, and Museums (GLAM) sector. Omeka-S allows for standards-led organisation and exhibition of digital materials. As opposed to most other web applications, it is not just a front-end to make content look appealing. It is also supported by archival metadata-driven back-end processes, enabling the re-use of materials via many other discovery platforms (Omeka-S Proposal Project Plan). Therefore, it is a repository and not a website because the backend of repositories allows for the creation of metadata and the creation of robust schemas that capture consistent metadata for each of the uploaded items.

5.1 Data Curation: Digitisation to Repository Publishing

As the material in the collection is over 20 years old, and UCT had gone through a phase of changes in personnel handling the digitisation process, as well as changes in the technologies employed for digitisation, a re-evaluation of the overall context was needed. Any kind of workflow that would lead towards a published repository therefore required consolidation, or a period of curation of the contents of the collection in line with new technological advances.

The legacy media is split between tapes using Digital Video (DV) and DVCAM (Sony's version of Digital Video) formats, a subset of which has gone through the transcription process (the entire collection also includes audio tapes as well as VHS). Previously, there was also a process of digitisation which led to derivatives of these tapes being captured on optical and hard drives. All of the legacy media material on the various forms of storage needed to be reconciled, organised and catalogued. It also needed to be analysed, by identifying and organising the content that would lead back to the central aim of the repository - to preserve the histories and the languages of the ǂKhomani San.

With this in mind, the curation component of the digitisation process involved not only looking at the media from an archival point of view, but also from a more conceptual perspective in terms of what was going to be showcased and for whom. How were visitors to the site going to interact with the different media? Who were the visitors going to be and what would they be looking for? Are the visitors going to be members of the ǂKhomani San community, and if so, how could the repository be arranged to make it accessible for them to navigate. Taking these requirements into account, as well as organising the media data, a further step was taken to organise the content of the data. For example, the development of spreadsheets to capture information such as: the full names of ǂKhomani San community members, place names and their associated GIS data, specifically mentioned cultural ceremonies, and indigenous plants for their edible or medicinal properties. All these variables needed to be identified and described in order to curate the media on a website and allow for multiple exploration points of the collection. This organisation of the data led to the grouping of distinct themes within the collection:

- PeopleCommunity
- PeopleContributors
- Places
- CulturalPractices
- Plants

And within each theme, the metadata used to describe it would be unique. For example:

- PeopleCommunity
    - name_second_surname
    - name_first_surname
    - name_first
    - name_traditional
    - name_nickname
    - name_housename
    - name_other
    - gender
    - birth_place
    - birth_date
    - death_place
    - death_date
    - biography

5.2 Challenges in Data Clean-up

The starting point for the creation of linked data rested within the 200+ transcripts that had been developed thus far (covering only a fraction of the entire audio-visual archive). The transcripts followed a similar layout within a Microsoft Word Document, and included a cell which was used to identify keywords related to the media (video tape). The keywords could relate to individuals on the video, other people, cultural ceremonies, locations, etc.

The first step was to extract the keywords cell from each of the 200 documents and place them in a structured table. This table of keywords provided metadata for the creation of records in the repository. In this way, when a media clip, i.e. 1998-05_12 was uploaded, it would be possible to "tag" it with the appropriate keywords that had been identified in the transcript. Having these keywords as tags would enable exploration of the collection.

The process of automatic extraction of the keywords from the 200 documents was enabled through the use of Python programming language which has built-in libraries to access components of a Word document. The code created a table with a column for the "clip name" and another column for the "keywords". With some data tools through the R programming language, it was possible to reframe the data in the format such as Table 3. In this instance, each unique keyword is in a new row and the columns alongside, list the names of the clips where those keywords are found.

However, with multiple individuals working on this collection over the years throughout several phases of the project to discover the data, the keywords became unavoidably inconsistent. While keywords were captured for every single tape, they were established by a number of different individuals without the building of a necessary controlled vocabulary. Therefore, multiple spelling variations arose, as well as more and more languages and their associated translations, resulting in a singular concept being captured in many different ways (see Table 3 - bat-eared fox). For any kind of machine or computer program each of these different spellings is a different concept. A website built upon such a list of keywords would not be able to provide paths to distinct people, places or concepts.

The challenge was then to consolidate these different spellings into single entries, so that when each of the clips were uploaded onto the exhibition site, they would point to a unique list of concepts or entries. This required the use of a digital tool called OpenRefine, which specialises in cleaning up "messy" data. In the example in Table 3 below, OpenRefine was able to identify that the five different spellings of "bat-eared fox" all refer to the same thing and consolidate the entries by combining the columns with the tapes being referenced as one line-item. This would result in the keyword of "bat-eared fox" being tied to distinct media items, enabling the user to journey through all of the clips which have it mentioned.

Keyword	Tape	Tape	Tape[...]
bat eared fox	1998_05-12		
bat-eared fox	1998_01_04	1997_07-13	2001_04-06
bat-eared foxes	1998_03-05		
bat-earred fox	1998_07-01	2000_02-07	1998_05-15
beard	1997_02-03		
beat-earred fox	2001_02-04		
beatig	2001_06-03		

Table 3: An example of data clean-up using OpenRefine to identify and group like entries for consolidation

This process of data clean-up in relation to the keywords found in the transcript files moved towards establishing a controlled vocabulary which could be used in future as further transcripts are added. This controlled process ensures the continual building of the collection by connecting to the existing dataset and forming immediate links. In other words, when a new tape is added, the keyword referring to a certain individual from that tape e.g. "|Una", would be tied to the existing vocabulary and therefore link the new media clip and its associated transcript file, to the existing data containing the same entry.

5.3 Multilingual Support

It was imperative to capture the multilingual and cultural fluidity of the community in the repository. This gives the option of linking data objects and is crucial to the creation of the digital collection and to the objectives of the project. The linked data capabilities of Omeka-S allow for singular concepts to be mapped out to different versions or expressions, allowing for multilingual support. For example, a search for a word (e.g. a place name) in any of the languages within the collection would link back to the same concept, object, or person that it refers to irrespective of the language used in the search

5.4 Navigating the Website

With respect to organising the media and the content on the collections' feature website, the site needed a number of different entry points. Omeka-S lends itself to multiple presentations, due, in large part, to the nature of the database of links that are formed as the items are uploaded. This means that complex webpages populated by diverse elements can be setup through a simple query, as opposed to any hard coding or laborious design and arrangement work. For example, by setting up a simple template and a query to list all elements which reference a specific individual, the Omeka-S software can generate a page that presents all of the various media elements, together with any captured metadata, as well as certain custom texts. It therefore becomes easy to navigate through the collection by spending time on a page dedicated to each individual community member and accessing the transcripts, photos, and videos in which they are present. This way of navigating can be repeated with any of the conceptual elements within the collection (places, cultural ceremonies, plants, etc), thanks to the established keyword vocabulary which allows for multiple expressions to tie to a singular item, i.e. a many to one relationship. This flexibility allows for example, a cultural ceremony to be explored from many different personal narratives, or a particular place to be referred to by more than one speaker, or a specific plant to have multiple uses.

Furthermore, the website can also be explored chronologically through the journeys of the researchers who built the original collection, looking through the media in sequential order. With a view towards a kind of meta curation, the website also has custom pages that draw on a few key items to deliver a more pointed story. An example of this builds upon the keywords that had been lifted from the transcript sheets, consolidated and then used as the keywords in the upload of each of the metadata items. Building upon the description in the previous paragraph, it would be possible to allow visitors to the website to search for specific individuals talking about specific cultural ceremonies, or to listen and view all those who talk about a specific physical location. These custom pages can then be built by the collection team and scaffold upon such queries from the collection to highlight specific issues or themes. These custom pages can continue to be built as more individuals engage with the collection and express their interests or concerns. Such individuals could be researchers or members of the community or general public. These custom pages can be composed of text that is written specifically for that page, and then placed alongside some of the media items, which may be related to people, places, cultural ceremonies or plants. A culmination of custom designed pages based on the user engagement with the content of the collection results in a unique and continuously evolving resource.

6. The Importance of Collaboration

Researchers from diverse fields were instrumental in collating all the relevant data required for a successful land claim through a cultural heritage audit. Such fields included: visual anthropology, law, linguistics, cartography, conservation and social development (as exemplified in Figure 6). Such an endeavour would not have been possible without the collaboration of ǂKhomani San community members, researchers from diverse fields, charity organisations, NGOs and Universities alike. Such unity in diversity of expertise is testament to a potentially new methodology that embraces a decolonial ethos for one of South Africa's most unique narratives.

Figure 6: Cartographer Bill Kemp, working alongside linguist Levi Namaseb and former leader of the ǂKhomani San, Dawid Kruiper to create detailed maps of significant places in Khoekhoe, Afrikaans and English

7. Summary

This paper highlights the social, historical and linguistic context of the ǂKhomani San | Hugh Brody collection with a particular emphasis on the digitisation process applied by the University of Cape Town's Digital Library Services to deliver an accessible end-product.

Until the final URL is available please contact Michal Singer, Special Collections, UCT Libraries, michal.singer@uct.ac.za for current access details to the collection or either of the authors of this paper.

8. Acknowledgements

This digital collection was made possible due to the input provided by the ǂKhomani San community, Hugh Brody, Open Channels, the South African San Institute, African Tongue, University of Fraser and the University of Cape Town Libraries.

9. Bibliographical References

Adamo, J. (2011). Omeka and the NLM Digital Repository: A New way of Creating HMD-Curated Websites. National Library of Medicine. (Online) Available: https://www.nlm.nih.gov/about/training/associate/associate_projects/AdamoOmekaReport2011.pdf

Crawhall, N. (2001). *Written in the Sand: Auditing and managing cultural resources with displaced indigenous peoples: A South African case study.* Mowbray: SASI.

Gruber, E. Building Omeka Exhibits with Fedora Repository Content. Published December 15, 2010. (Online) Available: https://scholarslab.lib.virginia.edu/blog/building-omeka-exhibits-with-fedora-repository-content/

Güldemann, T. (2008). Greenberg's "case" for Khoisan: the morphological evidence. In D. Ibriszimow (Ed.), *Sprache und Geschichte in Afrika, 19* (pp. 123-153). Köln: Rüdiger Köppe

Hardesty, J.L. (2014). Exhibiting library collections online: Omeka in context. (Online) Available: https://scholarworks.iu.edu/dspace/bitstream/handle/2022/17627/HardestyJulietL_ExhibitingLibraryCollectionsOnlineOmekaInContext.pdf;sequence=1

Heine, B and Honken, H (2010). The Kx'a Family: A new Khoisan genealogy. *Journal of Asian and African Studies*, 79: 5-36.

Jing, J. (2015). Digital asset management (dam) systems used in Libraries. Queen's University Library. (Online) Available: https://www.slideshare.net/happyrainb/digital-asset-management-dam-systems-used

Jing, J. (2016). The workflows for the ingest of digital objects into a repository/digital library. (Online) Available: https://www.slideshare.net/happyrainb/the-workflows-for-the-ingest-of-digital-objects-into-a-repositorydigital-library

Jones (2019). Contemporary Khoesan languages of South Africa. *Critical Arts.* DOI: 10.1080/02560046.2019.1688849

Kandybowicz, J., and Torrence, H., (2017). Africa's endangered languages: Documentary and theoretical approaches. New York: Oxford University Press.

Omeka-S. (Online) Available: https://omeka.org/s/

Penn Libraries Guides: Omeka. (Online) Available: https://guides.library.upenn.edu/omeka

Sands, B., Miller, A., Burgman, J., Namaseb, L., Collins, C., Exter, M., (2006). 1400 item N|uu Dictionary. Manuscript.

Statistics South Africa (2018). General Household Survey 2018. Statistical Release, P03182018, Available at: http://www.statssa.gov.za/publications/P0318/P03182018.pdf

du Plessis, M. (2018). Kora: A lost Khoisan language of the early Cape and the Gariep. Pretoria: Unisa Press.

Voβen, R. (2013). *The Khoesan Languages. Routledge Language Family Series*. London: Routledge.

Witzlack-Makarevich, Al. (2006). *Aspects of Information Structure in Richtersveld Nama.* MA thesis, Institut für Linguistik der Universität Leipzig.

Proceedings of the First workshop on Resources for African Indigenous Languages (RAIL), pages 9–14
Language Resources and Evaluation Conference (LREC 2020), Marseille, 11–16 May 2020

Usability and Accessibility of Bantu Language Dictionaries in the Digital Age: Mobile Access in an Open Environment

Thomas Eckart, Sonja Bosch, Uwe Quasthoff, Erik Körner, Dirk Goldhahn, Simon Kaleschke
Natural Language Processing Group, University of Leipzig, Germany
Department of African Languages, University of South Africa, Pretoria, South Africa
{teckart, quasthoff, koerner, dgoldhahn, skaleschke}@informatik.uni-leipzig.de
boschse@unisa.ac.za

Abstract

This contribution describes a free and open mobile dictionary app based on open dictionary data. A specific focus is on usability and user-adequate presentation of data. This includes, in addition to the alphabetical lemma ordering, other vocabulary selection, grouping, and access criteria. Beyond search functionality for stems or roots – required due to the morphological complexity of Bantu languages – grouping of lemmas by subject area of varying difficulty allows customization. A dictionary profile defines available presentation options of the dictionary data in the app and can be specified according to the needs of the respective user group. Word embeddings and similar approaches are used to link to semantically similar or related words. The underlying data structure is open for monolingual, bilingual or multilingual dictionaries and also supports the connection to complex external resources like Wordnets. The application in its current state focuses on Xhosa and Zulu dictionary data but more resources will be integrated soon.

Keywords: dictionary data, mobile application, usability

1. Introduction

Lexical data sets are an indispensable resource for a variety of user groups, ranging from school children to professional text creators. However, the traditional ways of presenting and distributing this valuable knowledge by means of printed books does not reach all potential users anymore. New ways of data access and participation have to be identified and implemented as part of their further development. Even though many relevant resources are already available via Web pages, recent trends to extended use of dedicated mobile applications (apps) especially by a younger audience are only considered to a small extent and have led to - if any - a variety of incompatible, proprietary and therefore - after some time - abandoned applications with unmaintained data stocks.

The mobile cellular community in Africa is a fast growing one. In the case of South Africa, it was reported by Statistics South Africa[1] that the proportion of households owning mobile phones significantly increased from 31.9% in 2001 to 88.9% in 2011, while a community survey in 2016 (Statistics South Africa, 2016) indicated a further increase to 93.8% of households. Mobile phones resorted under the category “household goods”, and interestingly enough, achieved the highest percentage after electric stoves, TVs, and fridges. Mobile versions of Bantu language dictionaries could therefore facilitate accessibility to a large percentage of the population in contrast to traditional dictionaries which are expensive, often out of print and even outdated. Such electronic dictionaries also save users time compared to paper dictionaries. Moreover, they “save working-memory for comprehension processing rather than being disrupted by taking much time finding words in traditional dictionaries” (Deng and Trainin, 2015:58).

Taking this general environment into consideration, this contribution focuses on an Android dictionary application designed as an open source project to enhance the visibility of available resources and as an attempt to reach and activate new user groups. It will be shown how available resources - in part compiled or prepared by the authors themselves - can be made accessible and how openness can help to achieve similar results for other resources as well. Based on the analysis of existing mobile applications and their shortcomings, some approaches to improve the presentation and accessibility of data on a limited screen will be depicted with a focus on (semi-)automatic approaches for less-resourced languages.

2. Openness as Prerequisite for Collaboration and Participation

The FAIR data principles (findability, accessibility, interoperability, and reusability; see Wilkinson et al., 2016) have a growing influence on the everyday work of researchers and scientists. However, this - in general accepted - focus on a minimal set of requirements for allowing modern and open research is still not implemented in all areas. The consequences are serious and problematic especially for disciplines where the availability of reliable resources itself is problematic. Among others, this is specifically the case for many African indigenous languages of which most can be considered as resource scarce.

To achieve an open environment where interested researchers and users can collaborate and develop resources continuously, the required level of “openness” does not only include the ability to find, access, interoperate, and reuse data. In the context of this contribution, the focus lies on a more complete scenario when providing access to lexical resources for Bantu languages. The following views on openness are of particular relevance here:

- Open data: The availability of data for research, aggregation, and for re-use in other contexts is an obvious prerequisite for an active community and continuous development of the language

1 http://www.statssa.gov.za

resources landscape. In this contribution, a Xhosa dictionary dataset that was previously made available by the authors under an open license (Bosch et al., 2018), is used. However, this only serves as a concrete example; a limitation to this specific dataset or Bantu language is not intended. The openness of data and compliance with general standards of their formal representation allow the integration of other resources as well, as already tested using resources from the Comparative Bantu Online Dictionary project (CBOLD[2]).

- Open application: Besides the focus on data respecting the FAIR principles, the reusability of applications is another important aspect. Open or free software[3] allows the reuse of applications for new purposes or data sets and their collaborative development and improvement. Therefore, the application presented here is made freely available[4] under an open source licence and can be reused by other interested parties.

- User-friendly application: The open availability of data via open user interfaces is only one prerequisite to attract users and potential collaborators. The user experience provided by an application and its appropriateness for relevant user tasks is another important precondition. Unfortunately, most of the current applications - including commercial apps - are only trying to transfer established paradigms of structuring and accessing dictionary data to the digital age. The following sections will focus on new approaches that are still feasible for the problematic field of less-resourced languages.

- User-friendly data import: To simplify the re-use of the application, the effort that is necessary to import other data sets should be kept as low as possible. This can be achieved in different ways: by relying on established standard formats and/or by providing a simple mechanism to feed data into the application that is applicable even for inexperienced users. The authors have decided to select a dual approach in which lexical data is provided in form of column separated value (CSV) files which can be created, maintained, and edited using standard office software (like LibreOffice or Microsoft Excel). For more elaborate and established formats, transformation procedures are provided. This currently includes transformation scripts for data structured according to the Bantu Language Model (BLM) which is based on the MMoOn ontology (Klimek, 2017). The support of additional formats is planned for the future.

- External open resources: No application can provide all available information for a language or incorporate all established and often very extensive external resources. However, direct links are a helpful feature and make use of the distributed landscape of language resources. In this context, referencing data of the African Wordnet (AfWN) (Bosch and Griesel, 2017) and the dynamic incorporation of extracted full-text material as usage samples (Goldhahn et al., 2019) via RESTful Web services (Büchler et al., 2017) is considered to be of high relevance.

Current endeavours towards integrated and open research infrastructures like the South African SADiLaR[5], the European CLARIN/CLARIAH (Hinrichs & Krauwer, 2014) and more can be seen as the natural context for all of these developments.

3. User Groups and Profiles

This general complexity of data access when based on a relatively simple data format should not restrict usability requirements. There is a variety of potential user groups such as language learners of different ages (pupils of different ages, adults), different skill levels (beginners, L1 and L2 learners, professionals), different tasks to accomplish (text reception vs. text creation), and different types of dictionaries (monolingual, bilingual or multilingual with different amount of details).

A single dictionary may address a single user group or multiple user groups. The combination of targeted user group and available data in the dictionary determine dictionary details presented to the user. For a given dictionary, the presentation for different user groups is defined by the dictionary data provider within the dictionary, ideally together with the dictionary author(s). The result is either a single interface option for a given dictionary or a selection of two or three different interfaces (for instance, for beginners or professionals), where the user can select the appropriate option. The interface definition applies both to macro- and microstructure. The macrostructure should be accessible to pre-select the lemmas shown to the user. In a usual dictionary, all lemmas are presented in alphabetical order. On this level, we have the option to restrict the set of lemmas (for instance, for beginners or to focus on specific subject areas) and to change their order.

For the microstructure, we can restrict the dictionary by ignoring some information which is assumed to be known to (or irrelevant for) the targeted dictionary user. This may include information in bilingual dictionaries which are in the user's mother tongue or information irrelevant for the specific task that the user tries to accomplish.

As a result, defined user groups have to be aligned to supported user profiles with direct consequences for the selection and presentation of lexical data. This alignment may be structured according to the following examples:

- For language learners, it is highly relevant to access words belonging to the same semantic field in a combined presentation. This may include vocabulary which is part of the same semantic field or - especially in the context of

2 http://www.cbold.ish-lyon.cnrs.fr

3 For the following definition of "free software": https://fsfe.org/about/basics/freesoftware.en.html

4Available at https://github.com/cheapmon/balalaika

5 https://www.sadilar.org

primary education - part of the same lesson. The selection of presented lemmas is also defined by users' abilities and might include the restriction to high frequent terms, basic vocabulary, or terms known from previous lessons. On the microstructure level, this might comprise a focus on translations and concrete usage examples, while reducing the amount of morphosyntactic information to a minimum.

- For professional writers a suitable user profile can be constructed accordingly. This might also include an exclusive focus on domain-specific vocabulary (omitting basic vocabulary completely), taxonomic information (like synonyms or antonyms), and references to external, additional sources for non-lexical information.

This focus on user profiles might be seen as an unnecessary restriction in comparison with the absolute flexibility of a user-driven configuration. However, the willingness of users to adapt an interface to their specific needs is often low, which is in clear contrast to the technical costs of providing this flexibility in an application. The reduction of options to a reasonable subset is seen by the authors as a viable compromise.

3.1 Approaches for Lemma Selection

Typically, on a smartphone display, a maximum of ten lemmas can be presented in addition to a selected dictionary entry. The selection of these lemmas is crucial for easy dictionary use. The standard solution is the selection of the alphabetically neighboring words in the lemma list. In many cases, there are more attractive alternatives:

- Alphabetical subselection by frequency: In a large lemma list, many infrequent words are contained. Especially a language learner might be interested in medium or high frequency words only.
- Alphabetical subselection by the dictionary compilers: Words may be marked by difficulty (as beginners vocabulary, for instance), or subject area (medicine, for instance). Each subset can be selected, and all other words are ignored in the lemma list.
- Semantically similar or related words instead of alphabetic order: Semantically related words can either be provided by the dictionary (as by Wordnet, for instance) or generated automatically by word embeddings like Word2Vec or similar approaches. See the following section for more details.

4. Lemma Selection Approaches for Less-resourced Languages

The approaches identified for an improved access and presentation of lexical data would typically rely on extensive, mostly manually created resources. This includes vocabulary lists for specific domains (like vocabulary relevant for different school lessons or fields of work) or extensive taxonomic data. Unfortunately, for less-resourced languages those are not always available.

One of the positive developments is the recent effort on creating African Wordnets[6]. Linking up with a Wordnet provides additional suggestions such as synonyms or related concepts, definitions and usage examples in order to provide more learning opportunities. The African Wordnets project is currently under development for nine Bantu languages spoken in South Africa. Currently the prototypical African Wordnet (AfWN) contains open source data of varying sizes for the nine official African languages of South Africa. The AfWN is closely aligned with the English Princeton WordNet (PWN)[7] which forms the basic structure for continual and manual expansion of the AfWN (Bosch and Griesel, 2017). This so-called expand method offers an established structure for building a new resource and is therefore usually preferred for less-resourced languages (Ordan and Wintner, 2007:5). This method requires translation of the PWN into the target African language.

There is also a variety of statistics-based approaches to enhance dictionary usability for the purposes identified above. Most of these can be seen as semi-automatic procedures that are able to generate candidates but still require manual inspection and approval. Currently, the following approaches are evaluated with respect to the problem of data sparseness that applies to all less-resourced languages.

4.1 Differential Wordlist Analysis

The analysis and comparison of word lists (Kilgarriff, 2001) has proven to be useful for a variety of applications, including the corpus-based extraction of domain- or author-specific vocabulary (Goldhahn et al., 2015). This can be used for the purposes sketched in this contribution as well.

As a specific show case, vocabulary was identified that is suitable for primary school children. The used approach relies on the comparison of relative word frequencies in domain-specific texts compared with the frequency in a more general reference text corpus. As domain-specific material, texts of the *Nal'ibali*[8] project were used. Nal'ibali is a campaign to promote a reading culture in South Africa and provides multilingual stories in 11 languages. A word list was generated using the Zulu texts (around 34,000 tokens) and compared with a reference corpus of around 15 million tokens provided by the Leipzig Corpora Collection (Goldhahn et al., 2012) that aggregates text material using Web crawling for hundreds of languages.

6 https://africanwordnet.wordpress.com
7 https://wordnet.princeton.edu
8 https://nalibali.org

The resulting word form list contains both function words and everyday vocabulary which can be used for vocabulary selection. As concrete examples, the following inflected terms were extracted: kakhulu (*very much*), umuntu (*person*), kusho (*say/mean*), ukudla (*food*), umama (*mother*), ubaba (*father*), izilwane (*animals*), unogwaja (*rabbit*). Figure 1 and 2 compare the presentation for ilanga (*sun, daytime*) in an alphabetical order using a complete Zulu dictionary (thus including unrelated lemmata having the same prefix) with its presentation among a subset of vocabulary, extracted from the same source.

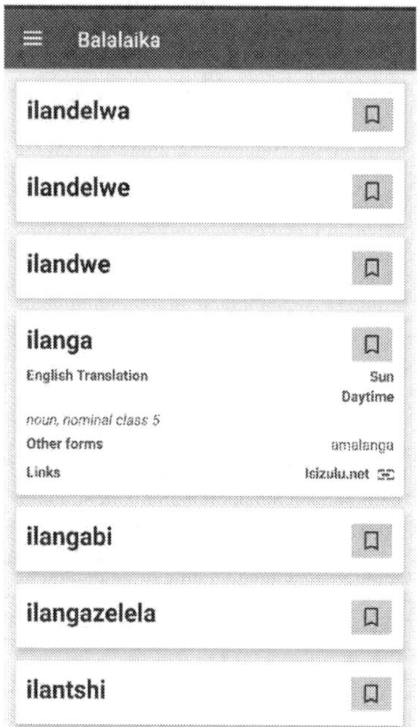

Figure 1: Zulu *ilanga* in an alphabetical lemma list

The sketched approach is of course not only usable for this specific kind of material, but can be applied to other genres as well. The basis in every case is a word list extracted from domain-specific texts. This can include school books, technical manuals, selections of Web pages or any other kind of text material.

4.2 Word Embeddings

The usage of word embeddings like Word2Vec (Mikolov et al., 2013) and Fasttext (Bojanowski et al., 2017) allows a variety of enhancements when using digital lexica. Their primary feature to compute semantic and/or syntactic similarity between two words can be used to provide different grouping options (clustering based on topic or similarity), suggestions of semantically related words and enables searching even with misspelled input words (Piktus et al., 2019). Word embeddings are comparable to word co-occurrences as they are both methods that exploit word contexts to "learn" the meaning of a word and related words. They are slightly more efficient to compute compared to traditional co-occurrences and can be stored more compactly which is helpful considering the limited amount of storage capacity on mobile devices.

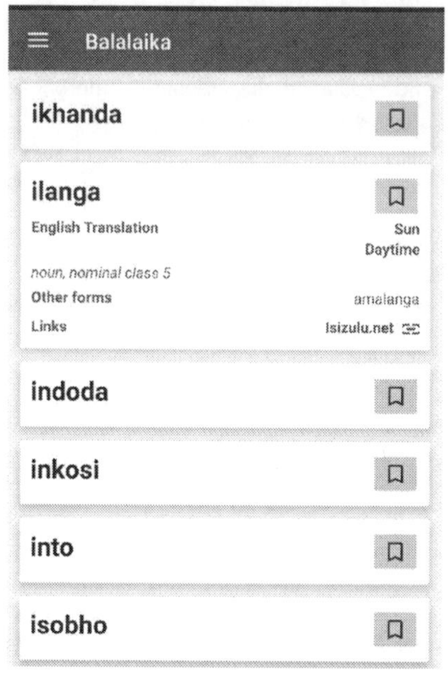

Figure 2: Zulu ilanga in a selection of domain-specific lemmata based on Nal'ibali texts (including *head, man, king, thing, soup*)

Different embedding techniques and models allow a choice between types of similarity, with Word2Vec focusing more on a kind of semantic similarity based on shared contexts, whereas Fasttext results are more morphologically similar as their calculation includes character n-grams, which is advantageous when working with unknown and infrequently occurring words. The choice of model can depend on language characteristics and user profiles. If possible, models should be trained on all available textual data for the given language. But even rather small text collections of about one million sentences allow for good results as shown below for Zulu. Training with even less data is possible but quality increases with more training examples.

A negative aspect for offline app usage is that the model size even for rather small corpora is between 100 MB and 1 GB and grows with the vocabulary size (related to the text corpora size). To minimize the initial app size, improvements such as pre-computing a fixed number of similar words for each vocabulary entry, on-demand downloading of (larger) models or word lists or even compressing embedding vectors (Joulin et al., 2016; Shu et al., 2017) can help mitigate this issue.

As concrete examples, the following two lexical items and their most similar forms in the dictionary according to (sub-) word similarity using Fasttext are provided. The results are based on a 1.1 million sentences Zulu corpus[9]; English translations are provided in brackets.

- **ukulangazela** (*to long for*): nokulangazelela (*and longing*), nokukulangazelela (*longing for you*), ukulangazela (*longing*), unokulangazelela (*you can look forward*), kunokulangazelela (*more longing*), enokulangazelela (*longing*), Ukulangazelela (*Longing*), ukulangazelela (*longing*), yikulangazelela (*look forward to it*), Ukulangazelele (*You longed for it*), wokulangazela (*of longing*), njengokulangazela (*as longing*), okulangazelele (*that longed for*), kulangazela (*longing*), akulangazelelayo (*that/which/who long for it/you*), ukulangazelele (*you long for it*), ikulangazelela (*he/she/it/ longs for it*), ezokulangazelela (*that will long for you/it*), engakulangazelela (*that can long for it/you*)

The above examples represent inflection of the same basic verb stem by means of a variety of affixes. The meaning of the intransitive verb stem -langaza (*have a longing*) is extended by so-called verbal extensions -el- and -elel- to change the meaning to a transitive one, i.e. -langazela (*long for*). Various prefixes feature in these examples, ranging from the infinitive noun class prefix uku- in the word ukulangazela (*longing/to long for*) to subject and object agreement morphemes i- and -ku- in the word ikulangazelela (*he/she/it longs for it*) and possessive morphemes as in wokulangazela (*of longing*), to mention a few.

- **ibhayoloji** (*biology*): ibhayotheknoloji (*biotechnology*), ibhayografi (*biography*), iMayikhrobhayoloji (*Microbiology*), ezebhayoloji (*of biological*), yibhayotheknoloji (*it is biotechnology*), Ibhayotheknoloji (*Biotechnology*), bhayotheknoloji (*biotechnology*), ngeradiyoloji (*with radiology*), ifonoloji (*phonology*), ithayithili (*title*), nakwibhayoloji (*and in biology*), kwebhayoloji (*of biology*), nethayithili (*and a title*), kwemayikhrobhayoloji (*of microbiology*), zebhayoloji (*of biological*), ngokwebhayoloji (*it is that of biology*), ibhaysikili (*bicycle*), zebhayotheknoloji (*of biotechnology*), ibayoloji (*biology*)

The results above all include nouns which at least display noun class prefixes. In some cases these are preceded by other prefixes such as the copulative morpheme yi- as in yibhayotheknoloji (*it is biotechnology*), and a possessive morpheme as in zebhayoloji (*of biological*). The majority of identified nouns belong to the same semantic context as the input word.

For further illustration, the noun imibuzo (*questions*) occuring in Figure 3 is a sample entry that is partially enriched with the words ukubuza (*interrogation/to ask*) and ukuphendula (*to reply*), which are both semantically related lexical items and were also extracted based on word embeddings.

9 https://corpora.uni-leipzig.de/en?corpusId=zul_mixed_2019

4.3 Handling Faulty Input

Faulty or misspelled input words, or even out-of-vocabulary words, are a major usability issue. Users expect even for an "invalid" input to return a meaningful result, so methods for handling those use-cases are necessary.

Figure 3: Xhosa dictionary entries partially enriched with references to semantically related terms (based on word embeddings)

Simple n-gram based methods can be used for searching for probable candidate words and suggesting those. A more comprehensive method is Fasttext (or more resilient word embeddings by Piktus et al., 2019), as it handles broken input rather well by using "sub-words" to infer embeddings for misspelled or unknown input words to then retrieve similar known words.[10] Single word embeddings in Fasttext are comprised of embeddings of variable length word n-grams and robust against slight changes in letters and work best with morphologically rich languages.[11] Prefixes and suffixes are more general in meaning due to their occurrence in many words in different contexts, stems however are more integral for the meaning as can be seen in the example above. That does not exclude semantically related words with completely different n-grams but those are ranked lower and additional post-processing may be necessary to only retrieve those words.

10https://fasttext.cc/docs/en/unsupervised-tutorial.html#importance-of-character-n-grams

11https://fasttext.cc/blog/2016/08/18/blog-post.html#works-on-many-languages

5. Conclusion

The sketched application is still under heavy development and therefore subject to changes. Its current state can already be examined at its public code repository; more extensive documentation about deployment or data import will be provided soon. A first feature-complete version can be expected by May 2020 and will incorporate the aforementioned data sets. In parallel, more approaches for improved access to and presentation of lexical data with a focus on less-resourced languages will be evaluated; suitable candidates will be implemented at a later stage.

6. Bibliographical References

Bojanowski, P., Grave, E., Joulin, A., and Mikolov, T. (2017). Enriching word vectors with subword information. *Transactions of the Association for Computational Linguistics,* vol. 5, pp. 135–146, Dec. 2017. Available: https://www.aclweb.org/anthology/Q17-1010, https://arxiv.org/abs/1607.04606

Bosch, S., Eckart, T., Klimek, T., Goldhahn, D., and Quasthoff, U. (2018). Preparation and Usage of Xhosa Lexicographical Data for a Multilingual, Federated Environment. In: Proceedings of the 11th International Conference on Language Resources and Evaluation (LREC 2018), Miyazaki, Japan.

Bosch, S. and Griesel, M. (2017). Strategies for building wordnets for under-resourced languages: the case of African languages. *Literator* 38(1). http://www.literator.org.za/index.php/literator/article/view/1351

Büchler, M., Eckart, T., Franzini, G., and Franzini, E. (2017). Mining and Analysing One Billion Requests to Linguistic Services. In: Proceedings of The IEEE International Conference on Big Data 2016 (IEEE BigData 2016), Washington DC, 2016, 5-8. DOI: 10.1109/BigData.2016.7840979

Deng, Q. and Trainin, G. (2015). Learning Vocabulary with Apps: From Theory to Practice. *The Nebraska Educator: A Student-Led Journal*. 29. https://digitalcommons.unl.edu/nebeducator/29

Goldhahn, D., Eckart, T., Gloning, T., Dreßler, K., and Heyer, G. (2015). Operationalisation of Research Questions of the Humanities within the CLARIN Infrastructure – An Ernst Jünger Use Case. In: Proceedings of CLARIN Annual Conference 2015, Wrocław, Poland.

Goldhahn, D., Eckart, T., and Bosch, S. (2019). Enriching Lexicographical Data for Lesser Resourced Languages: A Use Case. In: Proceedings of CLARIN Annual Conference 2019. Eds. K. Simov and M. Eskevich. Leipzig, Germany.

Goldhahn, D., Eckart, T., and Quasthoff, U. (2012). Building Large Monolingual Dictionaries at the Leipzig Corpora Collection: From 100 to 200 Languages. In: Proceedings of the Eighth International Conference on Language Resources and Evaluation (LREC 2012), Istanbul, Turkey.

Hinrichs, E. and Krauwer, S. (2014): The CLARIN Research Infrastructure: Resources and Tools for E-Humanities Scholars. In: Proceedings of the Ninth International Conference on Language Resources and Evaluation (LREC 2014), Reykjavik, Iceland.

Kilgarriff, A. (2001). Comparing corpora. International journal of corpus linguistics, 6(1), 97-133.

Joulin, A., Grave, E., Bojanowski, P., Douze, M., Jégou, H., and Mikolov, T. (2016). FastText.zip: Compressing text classification models. arXiv:1612.0365

Klimek, B. (2017). Proposing an OntoLex-MMoOn Alignment: Towards an Interconnection of two Linguistic Domain Models. Proceedings of the LDK workshops: OntoLex, TIAD and Challenges for Wordnets.

Ordan, N. and Wintner, S. (2007). Hebrew WordNet: a test case of aligning lexical databases across languages. *International Journal of Translation,* special issue on Lexical Resources for Machine Translation, 19(1):39–58. http://cs.haifa.ac.il/~shuly/publications/wordnet.pdf

Piktus, A., Edizel, N.B., Bojanowski, P., Grave, E., Ferreira, R., and Silvestri, F. (2019). Misspelling Oblivious Word Embeddings. Proceedings of the 2019 Conference of the North American Chapter of the Association for Computational Linguistics: Human Language Technologies, Volume 1, pp. 3226–3234. https://www.aclweb.org/anthology/N19-1326/

Mikolov, T., Chen, K., Corrado, G., and Dean, J. (2013). Efficient Estimation of Word Representations in Vector Space. Proceedings of Workshop at ICLR, 2013.

Shu, R. and Nakayama, H. (2017). Compressing Word Embeddings via Deep Compositional Code Learning. http://arxiv.org/abs/1711.01068

Statistics South Africa. (2016). Community Survey. Pretoria: Statistics South Africa. http://cs2016.statssa.gov.za/wp-content/uploads/2016/07/NT-30-06-2016-RELEASE-for-CS-2016-_Statistical-releas_1-July-2016.pdf

Wilkinson M.D., Dumontier M., Aalbersberg, I.J., et al. (2016). The FAIR Guiding Principles for scientific data management and stewardship. *Scientific data,* 3, 160018.http://dx.doi.org/10.1038/sdata.2016.18, https://dash.harvard.edu/bitstream/handle/1/26860037/4792175.pdf

Proceedings of the First workshop on Resources for African Indigenous Languages (RAIL), pages 15–20
Language Resources and Evaluation Conference (LREC 2020), Marseille, 11–16 May 2020

Investigating an approach for low resource language dataset creation, curation and classification: Setswana and Sepedi

Vukosi Marivate[1,2], Tshephisho Sefara[2], Vongani Chabalala[3], Keamogetswe Makhaya[4], Tumisho Mokgonyane[5], Rethabile Mokoena[6], Abiodun Modupe[7,1]
University of Pretoria[1], CSIR[2], University of Zululand[3], University of Cape Town[4],
University of Limpopo[5], North-West University[6], University of the Witwatersrand[7]
vukosi.marivate@cs.up.ac.za, tsefara@csir.co.za

Abstract

The recent advances in Natural Language Processing have only been a boon for well represented languages, negating research in lesser known global languages. This is in part due to the availability of curated data and research resources. One of the current challenges concerning low-resourced languages are clear guidelines on the collection, curation and preparation of datasets for different use-cases. In this work, we take on the task of creating two datasets that are focused on news headlines (i.e short text) for Setswana and Sepedi and the creation of a news topic classification task from these datasets. In this study, we document our work, propose baselines for classification, and investigate an approach on data augmentation better suited to low-resourced languages in order to improve the performance of the classifiers.

1. Introduction

The most pressing issues with regard to low-resource languages are the lack of sufficient language resources, like features related to automation. In this study, we introduce an investigation of a low-resource language that provides automatic formulation and customisation of new capabilities from existing ones. While there are more than six thousand languages spoken globally, the availability of resources among each of those are extraordinarily unbalanced (Nettle, 1998). For example, if we focus on language resources annotated on the public domain, as of November 2019, AG corpus released about $496,835$ news articles related to the English language from more than 200 sources[1]. Additionally, the Reuters News Dataset (Lewis, 1997) comprise roughly $10,788$ annotated texts from the Reuters financial newswire. Moreover, the New York Times Annotated Corpusholds over 1.8 million articles (Sandhaus, 2008). Lastly, Google Translate only supports around 100 languages (Johnson et al., 2017). significant amount of knowledge exists for only a small number of languages, neglecting 17% out of the world's language categories labelled as low-resource, and there are currently no standard annotated tokens in low-resource languages (Strassel and Tracey, 2016). This in turn, makes it challenging to develop various mechanisms and tools used for Natural Language Processing (NLP).

In South Africa, most of the news websites (private and public) are published in English, despite there being 11 official languages (including English). In this paper, we list the premium newspapers by circulation as per the first Quarter of 2019 (Bureau of Circulations, 2019) (Table 1). Currently, there is a lack of information surrounding 8 of the 11 official South African languages, with the exception of English, Afrikaans and isiZulu which contain most of the reported datasets. n this work, we aim to provide a general framework for two of the 11 South African languages, to create an annotated linguistic resource for Setswana and Sepedi news headlines. In this study, we applied data sources of the news headlines from the South African Broadcast Corporation (SABC) [2], their social media streams and a few acoustic news. Unfortunately, at the time of this study, we did not have any direct access to news reports, and hopefully this study can promote collaboration between the national broadcaster and NLP researchers.

Table 1: Top newspapers in South Africa with their languages

Paper	Language	Circulation
Sunday Times	English	260132
Soccer Laduma	English	252041
Daily Sun	English	141187
Rapport	Afrikaans	113636
Isolezwe	isiZulu	86342
Sowetan	English	70120
Isolezwe ngeSonto	isiZulu	65489
Isolezwe ngoMgqibelo	isiZulu	64676
Son	Afrikaans	62842

The rest of the work is organized as follows. Section 2. discusses prior work that has gone into building local corpora in South Africa and how they have been used. Section 3. presents the proposed approach to build a local news corpora and annotating the corpora with categories. From here, we focus on ways to gather data for vectorization and building word embeddings (needing an expanded corpus). We also release and make pre-trained word embeddings for 2 local languages as part of this work (Marivate and Sefara, 2020a). Section 4. investigate building classification models for the Setswana and Sepedi news and improve those classifiers using a 2 step augmentation approach inspired by work on hierarchical language models (Yu et al., 2019). Finally, Section 5. concludes and proposes a path forward for this work.

[1] `http://groups.di.unipi.it/~gulli`

[2] `http://www.sabc.co.za/`

2. Prior Work

Creating sizeable language resources for low resource languages is important in improving available data for study (Zoph et al., 2016) and cultural preservation. Focusing on the African continent, we note that there are few annotated datasets that are openly available for Natural Language Processing tasks such as classification. In South Africa, the South African Center for Digital Language Resources (SADiLaR) [3] has worked to curate datasets of local South African languages. There remain gaps such as accessing large corpora and data from sources such as broadcasters and news organizations as they have sizeable catalogs that are yet to make it into the public domain. In this work, we work to fill such a gap by collecting, annotating and training classifier models for news headlines in Setswana and Sepedi. As the data that we do find publicly is still small, we also have to deal with the challenges of Machine Learning on small data. Machine learning systems perform poorly in presence of small training sets due to overfitting. To avoid this problem, data augmentation can be used. The technique is well known in the field of image processing (Cubuk et al., 2019). Data augmentation refers to the augmentation of the training set with artificial, generated, training examples. This technique is used less frequently in NLP but a number of few studies applied data augmentation.

Silfverberg et al. (2017) use data augmentation to counteract overfitting where recurrent neural network (RNN) Encoder-Decoder is implemented specifically geared toward a low-resource setting. Authors apply data augmentation by finding words that share word stem for example **fizzle** and **fizzling** share **fizzl**. Then authors replace a stem with another string.

Zhang et al. (2015) apply data augmentation by using synonyms as substitute words for the original words. However, Kobayashi (2018) states that synonyms are very limited and the synonym-based augmentation cannot produce numerous different patterns from the original texts. Hence, Kobayashi (2018) proposes contextual data augmentation by replacing words that are predicted by a language model given the context surrounding the original words to be augmented.

As Wei and Zou (2019) states that these techniques are valid, they are not often used in practice because they have a high cost of implementation relative to performance gain. They propose an easy data augmentation as techniques for boosting performance on text classification tasks. These techniques involve synonym replacement, random insertion, random swap, and random deletion of a word. Authors observed good performance when using fraction of the dataset (%):1, 5, 10, 20, 30, 40, 50, 60, 70, 80, 90, 100, as the data size increases, the accuracy also increases for augmented and original data. Original data obtained highest accuracy of 88.3% at 100% data size while augmented data obtained accuracy of 88.6% at 50% data size.

[3]www.sadilar.org

3. Developing news classification models for Setswana and Sepedi

In this work, we investigate the development of a 2 step text augmentation method in order to be improve classification models for Setswana and Sepedi. To do this we had to first identify a suitable data source. Collect the data, and then annotate the datasets with news categories. After the data is collected and annotated, we then worked to create classification models from the data as is and then use a word embedding and document embedding augmentation approach. In this section discuss how data was collected as well as the approach we use to build classification models.

3.1. Data Collection, Cleaning and Annotation

Before we can train classification models, we first have to collect data for 2 distinct processes. First, we present our collected news dataset as well as its annotation. We then discuss how we collected larger datasets for better vectorisation.

3.1.1. News data collection and annotation

The news data we collected is from the SABC[4] Facebook pages. The SABC is the public broadcaster for South Africa. Specifically, data was collected from Motsweding FM (An SABC Setswana radio station) [5] and Thobela FM (An SABC Sepedi radio station) [6]. We scraped the news headlines that are published as posts on both Facebook pages. We claim no copyright for the content but used the data for research purposes. We summarize the datasets in Table 2. We visualize the token distributions in Setswana and Sepedi in Figures 1 and 2 respectively.

Table 2: News Data Sets

	Setswana	Sepedi
Corpus Size (headlines)	219	491
Number of Tokens (words)	1561	3018

Figure 1: Setswana Wordcloud

[4]http://www.sabc.co.za/

[5]https://www.facebook.com/MotswedingFM/

[6]https://www.facebook.com/thobelafmyaka/

Figure 2: Sepedi Wordcloud

As can be seen, the datasets are relatively small and as such, we have to look at other ways to build vectorizers that can better generalize as the word token diversity would be very low.

We annotated the datasets by categorizing the news headlines into: *Legal*, *General News*,*Sports*, *Other*, *Politics*, *Traffic News*, *Community Activities*, *Crime*, *Business* and *Foreign Affairs*. Annotation was done after reading the headlines and coming up with categories that fit both datasets. We show the distribution of the labels in both the Setswana and Sepedi data sets in Figures 3 and 4 respectively. For this work, we only explore single label categorization for each article. It remains future work to look at the multi-label case. As such, there might be some noise in the labels. Examples from the Sepedi annotated news corpus are shown next:

> *Tsela ya N1 ka Borwa kgauswi le Mantsole Weighbridge ka mo Limpopo ebe e tswaletswe lebakanyana ka morago ga kotsi yeo e hlagilego.*
> **Traffic**

> *Tona ya toka Michael Masutha,ore bahlankedi ba kgoro ya ditirelo tsa tshokollo ya bagolegwa bao ba tateditswego dithieeletsong tsa khomisene ya go nyakisisa mabarebare a go gogwa ga mmuso ka nko,ba swanetse go hlalosa gore ke ka lebaka la eng ba sa swanelwa go fegwa mesomong*
> **Legal**

The full dataset is made available online (Marivate and Sefara, 2020b) for further research use and improvements to the annotation[7]. As previously discussed, we used larger corpora to create language vectorizers for downstream NLP tasks. We discuss this next.

3.1.2. Vectorizers

Before we get into the annotated dataset, we needed to create pre-trained vectorizers in order to be able to build more classifiers that generalize better later on. For this reason we collected different corpora for each language in such as

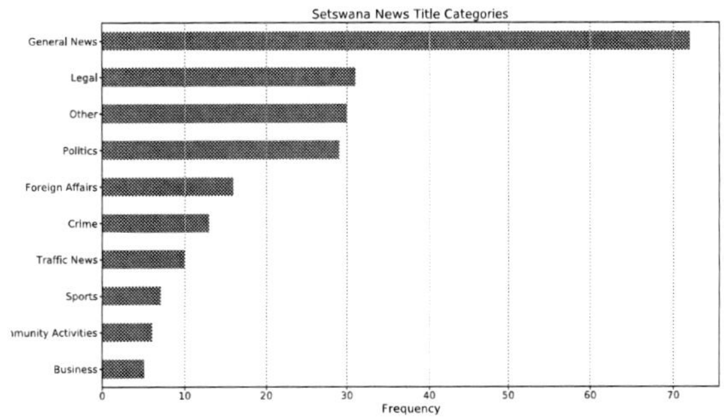

Figure 3: Setswana news title category distribution

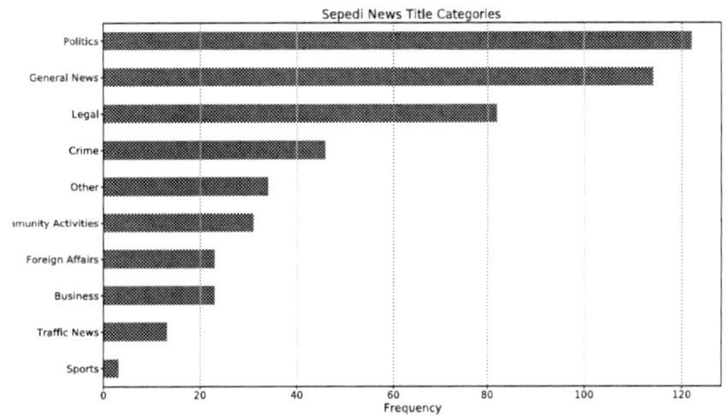

Figure 4: Sepedi news title category distribution

way that we could create Bag of Words, TFIDF, Word2vec (Mikolov et al., 2013) and FastText (Bojanowski et al., 2017) vectorizers (Table 3). We also make these vectorizers available for other researchers to use.

Table 3: Vectorizer Corpora Sizes in number of lines (number of tokens)

Source	Setswana	Sepedi
Wikipedia	478(*21924*)[8]	300(*10190*)[9]
JW300[10]	874464(*70251*)	618275(*53004*)
Bible	31102(*42233*)	29723(*38709*)
Constitution[11]	7077(*3940*)	6564(*3819*)
SADILAR[12]	33144(*61766*)	67036(*87838*)
Total	**946264(*152027*)**	**721977(*149355*)**

3.2. News Classification Models

We explore the use of a few classification algorithms to train news classification models. Specifically we train

- Logistic Regression,
- Support Vector Classification,
- XGBoost, and
- MLP Neural Network.

To deal with the challenge of having a small amount of data on short text, we use data augmentation methods, specifically a word embedding based augmentation (Wang

[7] https://zenodo.org/record/3668495

and Yang, 2015), approach that has been shown to work well on short text (Marivate and Sefara, 2019). We use this approach since we are not able to use other augmentation methods such as synonym based (requires developed Wordnet Synsets (Kobayashi, 2018)), language models (larger corpora needed train) and back-translation (not readily available for South African languages). We develop and present the use of both word and document embeddings (as an augmentation quality check) inspired by a hierarchical approach to augmentation (Yu et al., 2019).

4. Experiments and Results

This Section presents the experiments and results. As this is still work in progress, we present some avenues explored in both training classifiers and evaluating them for the task of news headline classification for Setswana and Sepedi.

4.1. Experimental Setup

For each classification problem, we perform 5 fold cross validation. For the bag-of-words and TFIDF vectorizers, we use a maximum token size of 20,000. For word embeddings and language embeddings we use size 50. All vectorizers were trained on the large corpora presented earlier.

4.1.1. Baseline Experiments

We run the baseline experiments with the original data using 5-fold cross validation. We show the performance (in terms of weighted F1 score) in the Figures 5 and 6. We show the baseline results as *orig*. For both the Bag-of-Words (TF) and TFIDF, the MLP performs very well comparatively to the other methods. In general the TFIDF performs better.

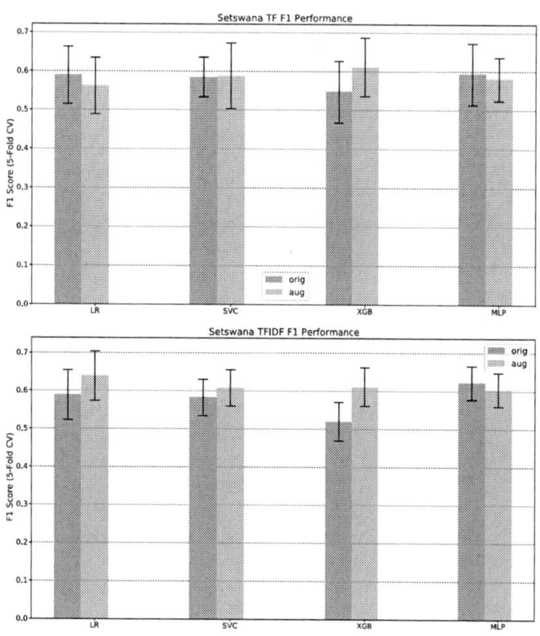

Figure 5: Baseline classification model performance for Setswana news title categorization

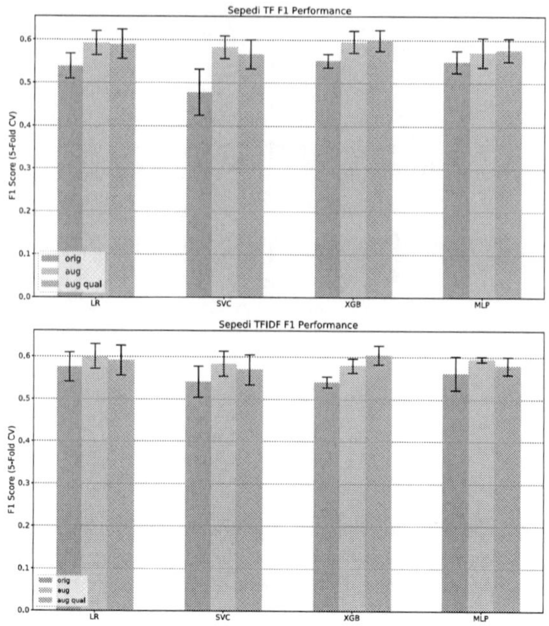

Figure 6: Baseline classification model performance for Sepedi news title categorization

4.1.2. Augmentation

We applied augmentation in different ways. First for Sepedi and Setswana word embeddings (word2vec), we use word embedding-based augmentation. We augment each dataset 20 times on the training data while the validation data is left intact so as to be comparable to the earlier baselines. We show the effect of augmentation in Figures 5 and 6 (performance labeled with *aug*).

The contextual, word2vec based, word augmentation improves the performance of most of the classifiers. If we now introduce a quality check using doc2vec (Algorithm 1) we also notice the impact on the performance for Sepedi (Figure 6 *aug qual*). We were not able to complete experiments with Setswana for the contextual augmentation with a quality check, but will continue working to better under stand the impact of such an algorithm in general. For example, it remains further work to investigate the effects of different similarity thresholds for the algorithm on the overall performance, how such an algorithm works on highly resourced languages vs low resourced languages, how we can make the algorithm efficient etc.

It also interesting to look at how performance of classifiers that were only trained with word2vec features would fair. Deep neural networks are not used in this current work and as such we did not use recurrent neural networks, but we can create sentence features from - word2vec by either using: the mean of all word vectors in a sentence, the median of all word vectors in a sentence or the concatenated power means (Rücklé et al., 2018). We show the performance of using this approach with the classifiers used for Bag of Words and TFIDF earlier in Figure 7.

The performance for this approach is slightly worse with

Algorithm 1: Contextual (Word2vec-based) augmentation algorithm with a doc2vec quality check

Input: s: a sentence, run: maximum number of attempts at augmentation
Output: $\hat{s}$ a sentence with words replaced

def `Augment` (s, run) :
  Let $\vec{V}$ be a vocabulary;
  for i **in** `range` (run) :
    $w_i \leftarrow$ randomly select a word from s;
    $\vec{w} \leftarrow$ find similar words of w_i;
    $s_0 \leftarrow$ randomly select a word from $\vec{w}$ given weights as distance;
    $\hat{s} \leftarrow$replace w_i with similar word s_0;
    $\vec{s} \leftarrow Doc2vec(s)$;
    $\vec{\hat{s}} \leftarrow Doc2vec(\hat{s})$;
    $similarity \leftarrow$ Cosine Similarity($\vec{s}$, $\vec{\hat{s}}$);
    if $similarity > threshold$:
      return($\hat{s}$);

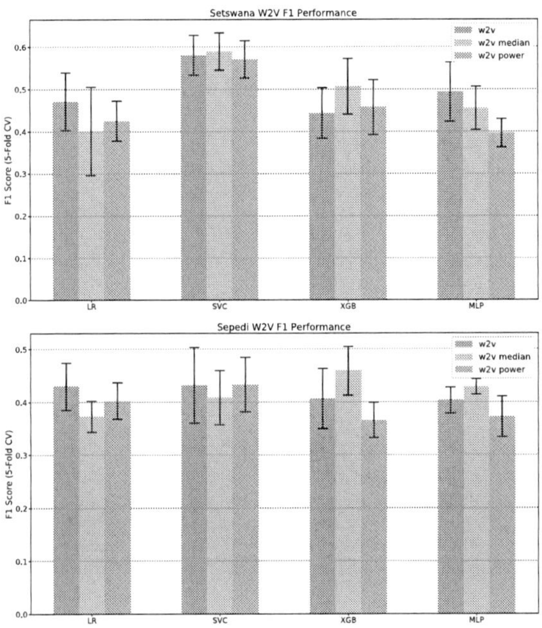

Figure 7: Word2Vec feature based performance for news headline classification

the best results for Sepedi news headline classification being with XGBoost on the augmented data. We hope to improve this performance using word2vec feature vectors using recurrent neural networks but currently are of the view that increasing the corpora sizes and the diversity of corpora for the pre-trained word embeddings may yield even better results.

Finally, we show the confusion matrix of the best model in Sepedi on a test set in Figure 8. The classifier categorizes *General News*, *Politics* and *Legal* news headlines best. For others there is more error. A larger news headline dataset is required and classification performance will also

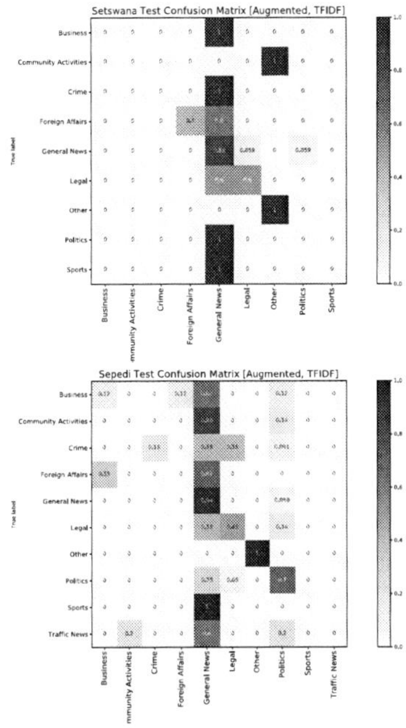

Figure 8: Confusion Matrix of News headline classification models

need to be compared to models trained on full news data (with the article body). For the Setswana classifiers, the confusion matrix shows that the data skew results in models that mostly can categorize between categories *General News* and *Other*. We need to look at re-sampling techniques to improve this performance as well as increasing the initial dataset size.

5. Conclusion and Future Work

This work introduced the collection and annotation of Setswana and Sepedi news headline data. It remains a challenge that in South Africa, 9 of the 11 official languages have little data such as this that is available to researchers in order to build downstream models that can be used in different applications. Through this work we hope to provide an example of what may be possible even when we have a limited annotated dataset. We exploit the availability of other free text data in Setswana and Sepedi in order to build pre-trained vectorizers for the languages (which are released as part of this work) and then train classification models for news categories.

It remains future work to collect more local language news headlines and text to train more models. We have identified other government news sources that can be used. On training embedding models with the data we have collected, further studies are needed to look at how augmentation using the embedding models improve the quality of augmentation.

6. Bibliographical References

Bojanowski, P., Grave, E., Joulin, A., and Mikolov, T. (2017). Enriching word vectors with subword information. *Transactions of the Association for Computational Linguistics*, 5:135–146.

Bureau of Circulations, A. (2019). Newspaper circulation statistics for the period January-March 2019 (ABC Q1 2019).

Cubuk, E. D., Zoph, B., Mane, D., Vasudevan, V., and Le, Q. V. (2019). Autoaugment: Learning augmentation strategies from data. In *Proceedings of the IEEE conference on computer vision and pattern recognition*, pages 113–123.

Johnson, M., Schuster, M., Le, Q. V., Krikun, M., Wu, Y., Chen, Z., Thorat, N., Viégas, F., Wattenberg, M., Corrado, G., et al. (2017). Google's multilingual neural machine translation system: Enabling zero-shot translation. *Transactions of the Association for Computational Linguistics*, 5:339–351.

Kobayashi, S. (2018). Contextual augmentation: Data augmentation by words with paradigmatic relations. In *Proceedings of the 2018 Conference of the North American Chapter of the Association for Computational Linguistics: Human Language Technologies, Volume 2 (Short Papers)*, volume 2, pages 452–457.

Lewis, D. D. (1997). Reuters-21578 text categorization collection data set.

Marivate, V. and Sefara, T. (2019). Improving short text classification through global augmentation methods. *arXiv preprint arXiv:1907.03752*.

Marivate, V. and Sefara, T. (2020a). African embeddings [nlp]. `https://doi.org/10.5281/zenodo.3668481`, February.

Marivate, V. and Sefara, T. (2020b). South African news data dataset. `https://doi.org/10.5281/zenodo.3668489`.

Mikolov, T., Sutskever, I., Chen, K., Corrado, G. S., and Dean, J. (2013). Distributed representations of words and phrases and their compositionality. In *Advances in neural information processing systems*, pages 3111–3119.

Nettle, D. (1998). Explaining global patterns of language diversity. *Journal of anthropological archaeology*, 17(4):354–374.

Rücklé, A., Eger, S., Peyrard, M., and Gurevych, I. (2018). Concatenated power mean word embeddings as universal cross-lingual sentence representations. *arXiv preprint arXiv:1803.01400*.

Sandhaus, E. (2008). The new york times annotated corpus. *Linguistic Data Consortium, Philadelphia*, 6(12):e26752.

Silfverberg, M., Wiemerslage, A., Liu, L., and Mao, L. J. (2017). Data augmentation for morphological reinflection. In *Proceedings of the CoNLL SIGMORPHON 2017 Shared Task: Universal Morphological Reinflection*, pages 90–99.

Strassel, S. and Tracey, J. (2016). Lorelei language packs: Data, tools, and resources for technology development in low resource languages. In *Proceedings of the Tenth International Conference on Language Resources and Evaluation (LREC'16)*, pages 3273–3280.

Wang, W. Y. and Yang, D. (2015). That's so annoying!!!: A lexical and frame-semantic embedding based data augmentation approach to automatic categorization of annoying behaviors using# petpeeve tweets. In *Proceedings of the 2015 Conference on Empirical Methods in Natural Language Processing*, pages 2557–2563.

Wei, J. and Zou, K. (2019). Eda: Easy data augmentation techniques for boosting performance on text classification tasks. In *Proceedings of the 2019 Conference on Empirical Methods in Natural Language Processing and the 9th International Joint Conference on Natural Language Processing (EMNLP-IJCNLP)*, pages 6383–6389.

Yu, S., Yang, J., Liu, D., Li, R., Zhang, Y., and Zhao, S. (2019). Hierarchical data augmentation and the application in text classification. *IEEE Access*, 7:185476–185485.

Zhang, X., Zhao, J., and LeCun, Y. (2015). Character-level convolutional networks for text classification. In *Advances in neural information processing systems*, pages 649–657.

Zoph, B., Yuret, D., May, J., and Knight, K. (2016). Transfer learning for low-resource neural machine translation. *arXiv preprint arXiv:1604.02201*.

Proceedings of the First workshop on Resources for African Indigenous Languages (RAIL), pages 21–24
Language Resources and Evaluation Conference (LREC 2020), Marseille, 11–16 May 2020

Complex Setswana Parts of Speech Tagging

Malema, G. Tebalo, B. Okgetheng, B. Motlhanka, M. Rammidi G.
University of Botswana
P/Bag 704, Gaborone, Botswana
{malemag,rammidig}@ub.ac.bw, {bokgetheng, mofenyimoffat}@gmail.com

Abstract

Setswana language is one of the Bantu languages written disjunctively. Some of its parts of speech such as qualificatives and some adverbs are made up of multiple words. That is, the part of speech is made up of a group of words. The disjunctive style of writing poses a challenge when a sentence is tokenized or when tagging. A few studies have been done on identification of multi-word parts of speech. In this study we go further to tokenize complex parts of speech which are formed by extending basic forms of multi-word parts of speech. The parts of speech are extended by recursively concatenating more parts of speech to a basic form of parts of speech. We developed rules for building complex relative parts of speech. A morphological analyzer and Python NLTK are used to tag individual words and basic forms of multi-word parts of speech respectively. Developed rules are then used to identify complex parts of speech. Results from a 300 sentence text files give a performance of 74%. The tagger fails when it encounters expansion rules not implemented and when tagging by the morphological analyzer is incorrect.

Keywords: parts of speech tagging, Setswana, qualificatives

1. Introduction

Setswana is a Bantu language spoken by about 4.4 million people in Southern Africa covering Botswana, where it is the national and majority language, Namibia, Zimbabwe and South Africa. The majority of speakers, about 3.6 million, live in South Africa, where the language is officially recognized. Setswana is closely related to Southern and Northern Sotho languages spoken in South Africa. There have been few attempts in the development of Setswana language processing tools such as part of speech tagger, spell checkers, grammar checkers and machine translation.

Setswana like other languages is faced with ambiguity problems as far as word usage is concerned and this has much impact in part of speech (POS) tagging. Text in the available resource Setswana corpus is not annotated and hence limited meaningful processing can be executed on the data in its current form. Setswana as a low resourced language is limiting corpus research pertaining to much needed significant amount of information about a word and its neighbours, useful in further development of other applications such as information retrieval, collocation and frequency analysis, machine translation and speech synthesis, among other NLP applications. Therefore, there is need to develop basic Setswana processing tools that are accurate and usable to other systems.

Parts of speech tagging identifies parts of speech for a given language in a sentence. The output of a POS tagger is used for other application such as machine learning, grammar checking and also for language analysis. The complexity of POS tagging varies from language to language. There are different approaches to part of speech tagging, the most prominent being statistical and rule-based approaches (Brants 2000, Brill 1992,1995 and Charniak 1997). Statistical approaches require test data to learn words formations and order in a language. They work well where adequate training data is readily available. We could not find a readily available tagged corpus to use. We therefore developed a rule based approach. Rule based techniques require the development of rules based on the language structure.

Setswana like some Bantu languages is written disjunctively. That is, words that together play a particular function in a sentence are written separately. For the sentence to be properly analysed such words have to be grouped together to give the intended meaning. There are several orthographic words in Setswana such as concords which alone do not have meaning but with other words they give the sentence its intended meaning. Some of these words also play multiple roles in sentences and are frequently used. Such 'words' includes include *a, le, ba , se, lo, mo, ga, fa , ka*. Without grouping the words, some words could be classified in multiple categories. This problem has been looked at as a tokenization problem in some studies (Faa et al 2009, Pretorius et al 2009 and Talajard and Bosch 2006)
Setswana parts of speech include verbs, nouns, qualificatives, adverbs and pronouns. Verbs and nouns are open classes and could take several forms. Studies in parts of speech tagging have concentrated on copulative and auxiliary verbs and nouns because of this (Faa et al 2009 and Pretorius et al 2009). Most of POS taggers have focused on tagging individual words. However, Setswana has POS in particular qualificatives and some adverbs that are made up of several words and in some cases about a dozen words (Cole 1955, Mogapi 1998 and Malema et al 2017). Setswana qualificatives include possessives, adjectives, relatives, enumeratives and quantitatives. Adverbs are of time, manner and location.
A few studies have been done on tokenization and parts of speech tagging for Setswana and Northern Sotho which is closely related to Setswana (Faa et al 2009 and Malema et al 2017). These studies have not covered tokenization of complex parts of speech. Adverbs, possessives and relatives have a recursive structure which allows them to be extended resulting in complex structures containing several POS. Complex in this case, we mean in terms of length and use of multiple POS to build one part of speech.
This paper investigates identification of Setswana complex qualificatives and adverbs using part of speech tagger. We present basic rules on how to identify complex POS such as adverbs, possessives and relatives. The proposed method tags single words and then builds complex tags based on developed expansion rules. The rules have been tested for

relatives and preliminary results show that most rules are consistent and work most of the time.

2. Setswana Complex POS

As stated above adverbs, possessives and relatives have a recursive structure that allow a simple POS to be extended into a complex POS. We have noted that in Setswana sentence structures, the verb can be followed by noun (object) or an adverb as also stated in the structure of Setswana noun and verb phrases (Letsholo and Matlhaku 2014). We have also noted that nouns could be followed by qualificatives. Thus a simple sentence could be expanded by stating the object the verb is acting on and how, where and when the verb action is performed. The object could be described by using qualificatives and demonstratives.
Examples:

mosimane o a kgweetsa (the boy is driving)
mosimane o kgweetsa koloi (the boy is driving a car)
mosimane o kgweetsa koloi ya rraagwe (the boy is driving his father's car)
mosimane o kgweetsa koloi ya rraagwe kwa tirong (the boy is driving his father's car at work)

The first sentence does not have an object. In the second sentence an object (*koloi/car*) is provided for the verb *kgweetsa(drive)*. In the third sentence, the object *koloi* is distinguished or modified by using the possessive '*ya rraagwe' (his father's)*. In the fourth sentence an adverb of place *(kwa tirong/at work)* is added to identify where the action (*kgweetsa/drive*) of driving is happening.
We have observed that possessives, relatives and adverbs have a recursive structure and therefore could be expanded using other POS to create a complex POS.

2.1 Possessives

Simple possessives are made up a concord followed by a noun, pronoun or demonstrative.

Examples:

kgomo ya kgosi (chief's cow)
kgomo ya bone (their cow)

In the first example above "*ya kgosi*" is the possessive, where *ya* is the possessive concord matching the noun class (class 9) of *kgomo(cow)* and *kgosi(chief)* is the root (noun in this case).
This is the simplest form of the possessive. However, the root can be expanded to form a complex possessive. The root can be other compound POS such as relatives, possessives, adjectives and adverbs. These compound roots could also be expanded using the sentence expansion rules as explained above. That is, if POS ends with a verb, the verb can be given an object and or an adverb in front of it and if the POS ends with a noun, the noun can be modified with a qualificative and or a demonstrative. The added POS could also be expanded in the same way recursively.
Examples:

koloi ya monna (the man's car)
koloi ya ntate yo o thudileng (the car that belongs to the man who had an accident)
koloi ya ntate yo o thudileng tonki (the car that belongs to the man who hit a donkey)
koloi ya ntate yo o thudileng tonki ya kgosi (the car that belongs to the man who hit the chief's donkey)
koloi ya ntate yo o thudileng tonki ya kgosi kwa morakeng (the car that belongs to the man who hit the chief's donkey at the cattle post)

In the first sentence *ya monna*, is just the possessive concord and a simple root (*monna/noun*). The second sentence expands the possessive by distinguishing the *monna(man)* with the relative, *yo o thudileng*. Since that relative ends with a verb we could give it an object, *tonki (donkey)* as done in the third sentence. The fourth sentence distinguishes the *donkey(tonki)* using another possessive, *ya kgosi*. The firth sentence adds an adverb of place, *kwa morakeng (at the cattle post)*, for the verb *thudileng (hit)*. Further expansion of the possessive could be done by providing objects and or adverbs for new verbs and modifying new nouns with qualificatives or demonstratives. In the last sentence "*ya ntate yo o thudileng tonki ya kgosi kwa morakeng*" is a possessive describing the noun *koloi*. This possessive is made up of a relative (*yo o thudileng*), noun (*tonki*), possessive (*ya kgosi*) and adverb (*kwa morakeng*). The main objective of this study is to develop ways to recognize such long/complex parts of speech.

2.2 Relatives

Relatives are made up of a concord and a root.
Example:

koloi e e thudileng (the car that had an accident)

e e thudileng is a relative, where *e e* is a relative concord for class 4 and 9 nouns and *thudileng* is the root. Using the same approach for expansion of verbs and noun we could expand this relative as follows.

koloi e e thudileng tonki (the car that hit a donkey)
koloi e e thudielng tonki ya kgosi (the car that hit the chief's donkey)
koloi e e thudileng tonki ya kgosi kwa morakeng (the car that hit the chief's car at the cattle post)

In the third example "*e e thudileng tonki ya kgosi kwa morakeng*" is a relative made up of a basic relative (e e *thudileng*), noun (*tonki*), possessive (*ya kgosi*) and adverb (*kwa morakeng*). The structure of examples above is referred to as direct relatives. Another category of relatives is known as indirect. Examples:

koloi e ba e ratang (the car they like)
koloi e a tla e rekang (the car she/he will buy)
ngwana yo Modimo a mo segofaditseng (the child that God blessed)
koloi

In this study we only looked at direct relatives which have a simpler structure compared to indirect relatives. Basic structures of Setswana qualificatives and adverbs could be found in (Cole 1955 and Mogapi 1998).

2.3 Adverbs

Adverbs could also be expanded when they use verbs and nouns. Examples:

kwa morakeng (at the cattle post)
kwa morakeng wa monna (at the man's cattle post)
kwa morakeng wa monna yo o berekang (at the cattle

post of the man who is working)

kwa morakeng wa monna yo o berekang kwa sepateleng (at the cattle post of the man who is working at the hospital)

kwa morakeng wa monna yo o berekang kwa sepateleng sa Gaborone (at the cattle post of the man who is working at Gaborone hospital)

The last example is an adverb made up of a basic adverb (*kwa morakeng*), possessive (*wa monna*), relative (*yo o berekang*), adverb (*kwa sepateleng*), possessive (*sa Gaborone*)

3. Implementation

Figure 1 below shows a block diagram of the proposed tagger. Individual words are first tagged using morphological and noun analyzers developed in Malema et al (2016 and 2018). Simple compound POS are then tagged using regular expression (RE) Python library from Python NLTK. Regular expressions for simple compound POS are used here. We developed regular expressions for adjectives, enumeratives and for basic forms of possessives, relatives and adverbs. In Malema (2017) a finite state approach was used to tag basic multi-word POS. In this study we used the Python NLTK regular expression library because it is faster and much easier to use. After identifying compound POS in a sentence, expansion rules are applied to each compound POS for possible expansion. These rules basically test whether the next word(s) could be part of the current POS.

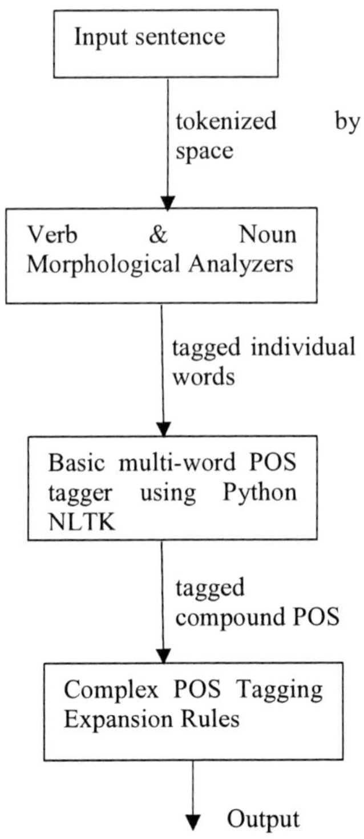

Figure 1: Block diagram of POS tagger

4. Performance Results

The proposed parts of speech tagger focused on complex direct relatives ending with a verb. The rule extensions developed are adding a noun, pronoun, qualificative, demonstrative or an adverb.

Examples:

ngwana yo o ratang (a child who likes ...)

ngwana yo o ratang go lela (a child who likes crying)

ngwana yo o ratang dijo (a child who likes food)

ngwana yo o ratang dijo tse di sukiri (a child who likes sweet food)

ngwana yo o ratang dijo tsele (a child who likes that food)

And so forth.

As the examples show we focused on the basic structure of direct relatives which is *Relative concord + Verb-ng*. This structure could be extended in a variety of ways

Concord + Verb-ng + N

Concord + verb-ng + T

Concord + verb-ng + P

Concord + verb-ng + D

Concord + verb-ng + Q

Concord + verb-ng + L

Where N is noun, *T* is a qualificative, *P* is a pronoun, *D* is a demonstrative, *Q* is a quantitative and *L* is an adverb.

The prototype tagger was given a 300 sentence text file from the Botswana Daily News (2019) and Mmegi (2019). The text file contains 123 relatives, 37 of which are of the basic form and the rest are more complex. The proposed tagger identified all the 123 basic relatives and successfully extended 64 of the complex relatives resulting with a success rate of 74%. The two main factors that lead to the failure of the tagger are:

Unexhausted Relative forms:

We noted that there are other forms that we have not included in this structure. For example, we noted that there are forms in which the verb is followed by '*ke*' and '*le*' which are not in our rules. Examples:

yo o salang le ngwana (the one who is baby sitting)

yo o rutwang ke mmaagwe (the one taught by his/her mother)

Failure of basic word tagging:

In some cases the morphological analyzer failed to tag verbs, nouns and adverbs(single word) properly which affected the regular expression tagger and the expansion rule application. Also in some cases nouns were not put in their correct classes. The concord(s) of a qualificative modifying a particular noun has to match with its noun class.

5. Conclusions

In this paper we presented a rule based approach to identifying Setswana complex parts of speech. The idea is to implement the recursive structure of complex parts of speech. The recursive structure is expressed in the form of rules which are based on simple verb and noun phrase structures. A prototype tagger was developed with the help of Python NLTK regular expressions. Preliminary results show that the proposed technique works well. However, for it to be effective, all the rules and structures of complex POS must be documented. In this study we did not exhaust all relative structures. We plan to develop the idea further by developing more rules and include other parts of speech.

6. Bibliographical References

Botswana Daily News (online), www.dailynews.gov.bw

Brants T (2000). A statistical part of speech tagger. *PANCL'00 Proceedings of the sixth conference on applied natural language processing Association for Computational Linguistics*

Brill E (1992). A simple rule based part of speech tagger. In *Proceedings of the third conference on Applied Natural Language processing, ACL,* Trento, Italy

Brill E (1995). Transformation Based Error-Driven Learning and Natural language Processing: A case study in Part of Speech Tagging. *Computational Linguistics*

Charniak E (1997).Statistical techniques for Natural Language parsin. *AI Magazine,* 18(4), pp.33-44

Cole, D.T. (1955). An Introduction to Tswana grammar. Longmans and Green, Cape Town.

Faa G, Heid U, Taljard E & Prinsloo D (2009). Part-of_Speech tagging of Northern Sotho: Disambiguating polysemous function words",*Proceedings of the EACL, 2009 Workshop on Language Technologies for African Languages – Aflat 2009*, pages 38—45, Athens Greece, 31 March 2009

Lombard, D.P (1985). Introduction to the Grammar of Northern Sotho. J.L. van Schaik, Pretoria, South Africa, 1985.

Louwrens, L. J.(1991). Aspects of the Northern Sotho Grammar. Via Afrika, Pretoria, South Africa.

Mmegi Publishing News paper (online: www.mmegi.co.bw

Malema, G, Okgetheng, B and Motlhanka, M. (2017) Setswana Part of Speech Tagging, International Journal of Natural Language Computing (IJNLC), Vol.6, No.6, pp. 15 – 20, December 2017

Malema, G. Motlogelwa, N. Okgetheng, B. Mogotlhwane O. (2016). Setswana Verb Analyzer and Generator. International Journal of Computational Linguistics (IJCL), Vol 7, issue 1, 2016.

Malema, G. Motlhanka, M. Okgetheng, O and Motlogelwa, N. (2018). Setswana Noun Analyzer and Generator. International Journal of Computational Linguistics (IJCL), Volume (9), Issue (2) pp 32—40, 2018

Mogapi, K.(1998). Thuto Puo ya Setswana, Longman Botswana, 184, ISBN:0582 61903 3.

Pretorius L, Viljoen B, Pretorius R and Berg A.(2009). A finite state approach to Setswana verb morphology, *International Workshop on finite state methods and natural Language Processing FSMNLP 2009: Finite State Methods and Natural language Processing,* pp. 131 – 138

Taljard, E. & Bosch, S. E. (2006). A comparison of approaches towards word class tagging: Disjunctively versus conjunctively written Bantu languages. Nordic Journal of African Studies, 15(4), 428–442.

Proceedings of the First workshop on Resources for African Indigenous Languages (RAIL), pages 25–30
Language Resources and Evaluation Conference (LREC 2020), Marseille, 11–16 May 2020

Comparing Neural Network Parsers for a Less-resourced and Morphologically-rich Language: Amharic Dependency Parser

Binyam Ephrem Seyoum, Yusuke Miyao, Baye Yimam Mekonnen
Addis Ababa University, University of Tokyo, Addis Ababa University
P.O.Box 1176, Addis Ababa, 7-3-1 Hongo, Bunkyo-ku, Tokyo 113-0033, P.O.Box 1176, Addis Ababa
{binyam.ephrem, baye.yimam}@aau.edu.et, yusuke@is.s.u-tokyo.ac.jp

Abstract

In this paper, we compare four state-of-the-art neural network dependency parsers for the Semitic language Amharic. As Amharic is a morphologically-rich and less-resourced language, the out-of-vocabulary (OOV) problem will be higher when we develop data-driven models. This fact limits researchers to develop neural network parsers because the neural network requires large quantities of data to train a model. We empirically evaluate neural network parsers when a small Amharic treebank is used for training. Based on our experiment, we obtain an 83.79 LAS score using the UDPipe system. Better accuracy is achieved when the neural parsing system uses external resources like word embedding. Using such resources, the LAS score for UDPipe improves to 85.26. Our experiment shows that the neural networks can learn dependency relations better from limited data while segmentation and POS tagging require much data.

Keywords: Dependency Parsing, Neural Network, Amharic

1. Introduction

Dependency parsing is the task of analyzing the dependency structure of a given input sentence automatically (Kübler et al., 2009). It requires a series of decisions to form the syntactic structure in the light of dependency relations. Nowadays, dependency grammar is gaining popularity because of its capability to handle predicate-argument structures that are needed in other NLP applications (Mcdonald et al., 2005). In addition, dependency grammar is recommended for languages that have free word order (Kübler et al., 2009; Tsarfaty et al., 2010). However, while dependency parsing is adaptable to many languages, it performs less well with morphologically rich languages like Arabic, Basque, and Greek (Dehdari et al., 2011). It is confirmed in (Habash, 2010), that languages like Arabic, Hebrew, and Amharic present a special challenges for the design of a dependency grammar due to their complex morphology and agreement.

Starting from the mid 20th century, research in NLP has shifted to neural networks. In this line of research, language is represented in the form of non-linear features. The approach is inspired by the the way computation works in the brain (Goldberg, 2017). It is applied in areas such as machine translation, computer vision, and speech recognition. With regards to parsing, the wave of neural network parsers was started in 2014 by Chen and Manning (Chen and Manning, 2014), who presented a fast and accurate transition-based parser using neural networks. Since then other parsing models have employed various techniques such as stack LSTM (Dyer et al., 2015; Kiperwasser and Goldberg, 2016), global normalization (Andor et al., 2016), biaffine attention (Dozat and Manning, 2017) or recurrent neural network grammars (Dyer et al., 2016; Kuncoro et al., 2017). Due to the existence of a treebank for different languages and the shared task of CoNLL 2017 (Zeman et al., 2017) and 2018 (Zeman et al., 2018), large improvements in dependency parsing using neural networks have been reported. For instance, the neural graph-based parser of Dozat et al. (Dozat et al., 2017) won the CoNLL2017 UD Shared Task. In the CoNLL2018 UD Shared Task, the winning system was that of Che et al. (Che et al., 2018). These systems have improved the neural network approach to parsing through the application of optimization functions and external resources such as word embedding. Nowadays, the state-of-the-art in parsing is neural networks incorporating word embedding.

In this paper, we present our experiment on developing a dependency parser for Amharic using the state-of-the-art method. The remaining sections are structured as follows. Section 2 gives a brief background about the process of developing the Amharic treebank and describes the treebank we used for training the neural network models. Section 3 describes the neural parsing systems we use to developed the parser. Section 4 presents our comparison and the results we obtained. The final section, Section 5, summarizes and points out the future directions of the research.

2. Background

A parsing system may use a model which is learned from a treebank to predict the grammatical structure for new sentences. This method of parser development is called data-driven parsing. The goal of data-driven dependency parsing is to learn to accurately predict dependency graphs from the treebank. Following the universal dependency (UD) guidelines, Binyam et al. (Seyoum et al., 2018) developed a treebank for Amharic. In building this resource, they followed a pipeline process. Clitics like prepositions, articles, negation operators, etc. were segmented manually from their host. Then the segmented data were annotated for POS, morphological information and syntactic dependencies based on the UD annotation schema.

The Amharic treebank (ATT) version 1 contains 1,074 manually-annotated sentences (5,245 tokens or 10,010 words). The sentences were collected from grammar books, biographies, news, and fictional and religious texts. The researchers made an effort to include different types of sentences. The data is included in the UD website[1].

3. Neural Network Parsers

In recent years, many fast and accurate dependency parsers have been made available publicly. Due to the shared task on dependency parsing and the presence of treebanks for different languages, every year new parsing methods have been introduced (Lavelli, 2016; Zeman et al., 2017). Some of the systems require a lot of resources and large treebanks while others are easy to adapt to new languages that have few resources. With this background, we have selected four off-the-shelf parsing systems to test for Amharic. The systems are: UDPipe[2], JPTDP[3], UUParser[4] and Turku[5].

3.1. UDPipe

UDPipe is an open-source and a trainable pipeline parsing system. It performs sentence segmentation, tokenization, part-of-speech tagging, lemmatization, morphological analysis, and dependency parsing (Straka et al., 2016). After a model is trained on the CoNLL-U format, it performs both sentence segmentation and tokenization jointly using a single-layer bidirectional Gated recurrent unit (GRU) network (Straka et al., 2017). The tasks of POS tagging, lemmatization, and morphological analysis, are performed using the MorphoDiTa of (Straková et al., 2014).
The parsing system of UDPipe is based on *Parsito*, (Straková et al., 2014) a transition-based system which is able to parse both non-projective and projective sentences. For non-projective sentences, it employs the arc-standard system of Nivre (Nivre, 2014). To handle non-projective sentences, it has an extra transition called "swap" that reorders two words. It uses neural network classifiers to predict correct transitions. For the purpose of improving parsing accuracy, it adds search-based oracles. It also includes optional beam search decoding, similar to that of Zhang and Nivre (Zhang and Nivre, 2011).

3.2. jPTDP

jPTDP is a joint model for part-of-speech (POS) tagging and dependency parsing (Nguyen and Verspoor, 2018). It was released in two versions; for our experiment, we used the latest version, jPTDP v2.0. This model is based on the BIST graph-based dependency parser of Kiperwasser and Goldberg (Kiperwasser and Goldberg, 2016). Given word tokens in an input sentence, the tagging component uses a BiLSTM to learn latent feature vectors representing the tokens. Then the tagging component feeds these feature vectors into a multi-layer perceptron (MLP) with one hidden layer to predict POS tags.
The parsing component uses another BiLSTM to learn a set of latent feature representations which are based on both the input tokens and the predicted POS tags. These representations are fed to one MLP to decode dependency arcs and another MLP to label the predicted dependency arcs.

3.3. UUParser

UUParser (version 2.3) is a pipeline system for dependency parsing that consists of three components (de Lhoneux et al., 2017). The first component performs joint word and sentence segmentation, the second predicts POS tags and morphological features, and the third predicts dependency relation from the words and the POS tags (Nivre, 2008). The word and sentence segmentation is jointly modeled as character-level sequence labeling, employing bidirectional recurrent neural networks (BiRNN) together with CRF (de Lhoneux et al., 2017).
The predictions of POS tags and morphological features are accomplished using a Meta-BiLSTM model with context-sensitive token encoding. This method is adopted from the work of Bohnet et al. (Bohnet et al., 2018). The method applies BiLSTM to modeling both words and characters at the sentence level, giving the model access to the sentence context. The character and word models are combined in the Meta-BiLSTMs. In the Meta-BiLSTM, they concatenate the output, for each word, (of its context sensitive character and word-based embedding) and pass to another BiLSTM to create an additional combined context sensitive encoding. This is followed by a final MLP, whose output is passed onto a linear layer for POS tag prediction.
The third component is dependency parsing, in which a greedy transition-based parser (Nivre, 2008) is applied, following the framework of Kiperwasser and Goldberg (Kiperwasser and Goldberg, 2016). The framework learns representations of tokens in context using BiLSTM. Both the token context and the transition (arc labels) are trained together with a multi-layer perceptron. This enables the model to predict transition and arc labels based on a few BiLSTM vectors. The authors also introduce a static-dynamic oracle, which allows the parser to learn from non-optimal configurations at training time.

3.4. Turku Parser

Turku is a neural parsing pipeline for segmentation, morphological tagging, dependency parsing and lemmatization (Kanerva et al., 2018). For sentence segmentation and tokenization, the system relies on the output of UDPipe. The pipeline allows pre-trained embeddings to be included in the training.
The tagging is done using the system of Dozat et al. (Dozat et al., 2017) which applies a time-distributed affine classifier to the tokens within a sentence. Tokens are first embedded with a word encoder. The encoder sums up a learned token embedding, a pre-trained token embedding, and a token embedding encoded from the sequence of its characters using a unidirectional LSTM. Next, a bidirectional LSTM reads the sequence of embedded tokens in a sentence to create a context-sensitive token representations. These representations are then transformed with ReLU layers separately for each affine tag classification layer (namely UPOS and XPOS). These two classification layers are trained jointly by summing their cross-entropy losses.
Lemmatization is another pipeline in the Turku parser in which the researchers develop their own lemmatization component. The system considers lemmatization as a sequence-to-sequence translation problem. They consider

[1]https://universaldependencies.org/
[2]https://ufal.mff.cuni.cz/udpipe
[3]https://github.com/datquocnguyen/jPTDP
[4]https://github.com/UppsalaNLP/uuparser
[5]https://turkunlp.org/Turku-neural-parser-pipeline

a word as an input, a sequence of characters which are concatenated with a sequence of its part-of-speech and morphological tags. The output is based on the corresponding lemma represented as a sequence of characters. The researchers essentially train their system to translate the word form characters and morphological tags into lemma characters. They use a deep attention encoder-decoder network with a two-layered bidirectional LSTM encoder for reading the sequence of input characters and morphological tags. As a result, they obtained vectors for the sequence encoder. During the decoding phase, they applied beam search with a size five.

The task of syntactic labeling in the Turku parser is based on the system developed by Dozat et al. (Dozat et al., 2017). The researchers follow methods similar to those that they implemented for the POS tagging module, where tokens were embedded with a word encoder. The word encoder, then, sums up the learned token embedding, a pre-trained token embedding, and a token embedding encoded from the sequence of its characters using unidirectional LSTM. The embedded tokens are then concatenated together with respective POS embeddings. BiLSTM then reads the sequence of embedded tokens in a sentence so that the system has context-aware token representations. The token representations are then transformed using four different ReLU layers separately for two different biaffine classifiers. The classifier scores possible relations (HEAD) and their dependency types (DEPREL), and best predictions are later decoded to form a tree. These relations and type classifiers are again trained jointly by summing up their cross entropy losses. Refer to (Dozat and Manning, 2017) and (Dozat et al., 2017) for the detailed process.

4. Comparing the Neural Network Parsers

Before we discuss the comparison, we describe the experimental set up we followed. The standard practice of preparing data is to divide the data into training, development and test set, usually 80 percent for training, and 10 percent each for development and testing. However, the data set we have is too small to be divided into such proportions. Instead, we carry out ten-fold cross-validation (Zeman et al., 2017), randomly selecting and grouping an equal number of sentences into ten sets. The data we used for this paper are freely available at http://github.com/Binyamephrem/Amharic-treebank. During the training phase, the data in the nine sets are used as a training set and tested against the sentences in the remaining set.

4.1. Experimental Results

In Table 1, we present the results of evaluating the parsing systems we trained. In order to make the evaluation fair, the first experiment is conducted by excluding other external resources. Since the Turku parser requires a pre-trained word embedding, we exclude it from this comparison. For evaluation purposes, we use the conllu18 evaluation script [6], which requires the data to be in the CoNLL-U format and gives us evaluation results for ULA, LAS, MLAS, and BLEX by comparing the system output with the gold data.

Parser	UAS	LAS	MLAS	BLEX
UDPipe	**95.16**	**83.79**	**76.33**	**79.00**
jPTDP	92.42	79.68	69.83	73.83
UUParser	92.00	79.47	70.30	73.66

Table 1: Comparison of the parsing systems

In all measures, UDPipe outperforms both jPTDP and UUParser. LAS computes the percentage of words that are assigned as both the correct syntactic head and the correct dependency label. A system with a higher LAS result will also have a higher result in other measures as well. However, a significant difference is observed in MLAS score (6.03-6.50). MLAS specifically focuses on the combined evaluation of both UPOS and morphological features. Both UDPipe and UUParser are pipeline systems whereas jPTDP is a joint model. The score of jPTDP on MLAS is worse, probably because the model focuses on POS tagging and dependency labeling only. Thus, it may be unjustifiable to compare them on this score as jPTDP does not consider morphological tags in the model. The same logic is applicable regarding the BLEX score. BLEX focuses on the relations between content words by considering lemmas, which are not modeled in jPTDP. The score we obtained for jPTDP probably results from the system seeing gold lemmas or the input data.

4.2. Parsing Model Enhanced with External Resources

We carried out another experiment in which models can be enhanced by external resources. One way of enhancing a model is to use a pre-trained word embedding. For this purpose, we used the trained model for Amharic using fasttext[7]. The data for training the model is from Wikipedia and Common Crawl[8]. The models were trained using continuous bag of words (CBOW) with position-weights, in dimension 300 and considered character of n-grams of length 5 with a window of size 5 and 10 negatives (Grave et al., 2018).

In this comparison, we have included the Turku parser as it requires a pre-trained word embedding. Table 2 presents the results when each model is enhanced with word embedding.

Parser	UAS	LAS	MLAS	BLEX
UDPipe	**96.00**	**85.26**	**77.90**	**80.73**
jPTDP	93.79	82.00	71.42	76.61
UUParser	93.26	79.89	70.65	74.18
Turku	93.26	81.79	68.67	77.36

Table 2: Model enhanced with pre-trained word embedding

We may observe that a pre-trained word embedding increases the performance of the model in each system. The percentage of improvement varies depending the system. jPTPD scores better in all measures, which indicates that the system benefits from the pre-trained model.

[6]http://universaldependencies.org/conll18/conll18_ud_eval.py

[7]https://fasttext.cc/docs/en/crawl-vectors.html

[8]http://commoncrawl.org

For instance, there is a 2.32% improvement over the LAS measure, which could be attributed to the small treebank used in the experiment. Another reason for the greater improvement of the jPTPD model might be related to "unknown" word representation, which are common in morphologically-rich languages. jPTPD uses character-based representations based on LSTM, which produces embeddings from a sequence of characters. This confirms that a character model is better for morphologically-rich languages with high type-token ratios (Smith et al., 2018). Since the UDPipe achieves better results in the first place, the increase due to word embeddings is naturally lower. Such improvements are sometimes evaluated using relative error reduction. For UDPipe, the relative error reduction is [9] approximately $\sim 9\%$. This means that 9% of the errors of the system without word embeddings are reduced using word embedding. Similarly, the relative error reduction for jPTDP is [10] $\sim 11.4\%$. Even by this measure, UDPipe did not benefit as much as jPTDP.

	Plain		segmented	
Metric	**UDPipe**	**Turku**	**UDPipe**	**Turku**
Token	100.00	99.70	100.00	100.00
Sentences	98.62	98.62	100.00	100.00
Words	80.23	80.07	100.00	100.00
UPOS	75.94	77.14	100.00	95.89
XPOS	75.38	76.91	100.00	94.95
UFeats	73.69	74.24	100.00	93.16
AllTags	72.23	74.66	100.00	90.84
Lemmas	80.23	80.07	100.00	100.00
UAS	62.08	61.60	95.16	93.26
LAS	55.32	55.63	83.79	81.79
CLAS	49.33	49.96	78.87	77.36
MLAS	42.74	46.06	76.21	68.67
BLEX	49.33	49.96	78.87	77.36

Table 3: Plain text and segmented text

4.3. Effect of the pipeline on the parsing system

Another experiment we conducted concerns the effect of each pipeline on the performance of the parsers when the input is plain text. For this purpose, we use both UDPipe and the Turku Parser. The remaining parsers need a separate segmentation model or input in CoNLL-U format. We compare the segmentation, tagging and parsing scores of both parsers. Table 3 presents the scores of each system when the input is plain text and segmented text.

We notice that there is a large gap in LAS between the gold and predicted segmentation. This may be caused by poor word predictions, which in turn lowers the tagging prediction. Token and sentence segmentation scores are high for both parsers. However, word segmentation scores for both parsers dropped significantly from 98% to 80%. The tagging result for the Turku parser is better when using gold segmentation (93-95%), but a huge decrease is observed (74-77%) when using predicted segmentation (or plain text). As a result of this, dependency attachment scores also significantly decrease(42â62%). This proves that error propagating in each pipeline greatly affects the attachment scores.

We may also notice from Table 3 that for UDPipe with the segmented input, the system is apparently using the gold POS and morphological features (scores are 100%). Thus, these numbers cannot be compared to the Turku pipeline. For the same reason, LAS scores for Turku with segmented input and UDPipe with segmented input cannot be compared. There is always an improvement when the parser can access gold tags and morphological tags. If there is a perfect tokenizer and tagger, better LAS scores can be obtained. Even though the Turku parser uses the segmentation model from UDPipe, the tagging scores for Turku are slightly better than for UDPipe when plain text is given to both systems.

5. Summary and Future Directions

This paper has presented a comparison of neural network parsers. Based on our comparison, we obtained an LAS score of 83.79 using the UDPipe system. This can be enhanced to 85.26 with external resources, i.e., word embedding. From the experiments we can recommend what will work better for Amharic. A parser for Amharic requires a segmentation of clitics before tagging. For this task, we recommend UDPipe. However, the performance of the segmentation need to be enhanced as it affects the tagging and attachment accuracy greatly.

We have compared both pipeline and joint models for tagging and syntactic parsing. From the pipeline systems, the Turku parsing system achieves better results in the tagging task. However, we have noted that parsing systems that follow the pipeline approach need to have a more efficient segmentation and tagging module. Since errors propagate from one pipeline to another, the parsing or dependency attachment is severely affected. If a joint model is preferred, one needs to consider morphological tagging in addition to POS tagging. Our experiment shows that the joint model is a promising research area for further studies. The jPTDP only focuses on POS and attachment information.

We intend to further our research in two ways. Since the data that the segmentation model was trained on was very limited, we plan to expand the data so that the model for segmentation can be enhanced. We can use the current segmentation prediction on a larger dataset and manually correct the predicted segmentation so as to have a better segmentation model. In addition, we will investigate the effect of learning a joint model of morphological tagging in addition to POS tagging and dependency attachment.

We conclude that, even though we have a small treebank, we can still develop a reasonably efficient parser for Amharic. That is, syntactic patterns can be learned from a small treebank. However, the data in the treebank needs to be carefully selected to include existing syntactic patterns in the language. The challenging aspect in future research will be learning the tags for new lexical items.

6. Bibliographical References

Andor, D., Alberti, C., Weiss, D., Severyn, A., Presta, A., Ganchev, K., Petrov, S., and Collins, M. (2016). Globally Normalized Transition-Based Neural Networks. *As-*

[9]It is calculated as (85.26-83.79) / (100-83.79)

[10]It is calculated as (82.00-79.68) / (100-79.68)

sociation for Computational Linguistics, arXiv preprint arXiv:1603.06042.

Bohnet, B., McDonald, R., Simoes, G., Andor, D., Pitler, E., and Maynez, J. (2018). Morphosyntactic Tagging with a Meta-BiLSTM Model over Context Sensitive Token Encodings. In *Proceedings of the 56th Annual Meeting of the Association for Computational Linguistics (Long Papers)*, pages 2642–2652, Melbourne, Australia. Association for Computational Linguistics.

Che, W., Liu, Y., Wang, Y., Zheng, B., and Liu, T. (2018). Towards Better UD Parsing: Deep Contextualized Word Embeddings, Ensemble, and Treebank Concatenation. In *Proceedings of the CoNLL 2018 Shared Task: Multilingual Parsing from Raw Text to Universal Dependencies*, pages 55–64.

Chen, D. and Manning, C. D. (2014). A Fast and Accurate Dependency Parser using Neural Networks. In *Proceedings of the 2014 Conference on Empirical Methods in Natural Language Processing (EMNLP)*, pages 740–750, Doha, Qatar.

de Lhoneux, M., Shao, Y., Basirat, A., Kiperwasser, E., Stymne, S., Goldberg, Y., and Nivre, J. (2017). From raw text to universal dependencies-look, no tags! In *Proceedings of the CoNLL 2017 Shared Task: Multilingual Parsing from Raw Text to Universal Dependencies*, pages 207–217.

Dehdari, J., Tounsi, L., and van Genabith, J. (2011). Morphological Features for Parsing Morphologically-rich Languages: A Case of Arabic. In *Proceedings of the 2nd Workshop on Statistical Parsing of Morphologically-Rich Languages (SPMRL 2011)*, pages 12–21, Dublin, Ireland. Association for Computational Linguistics.

Dozat, T. and Manning, C. D. (2017). Deep Biaffine Attention for Neural Dependency Parsing. In *ICLR2017*.

Dozat, T., Qi, P., and Manning, C. D. (2017). Stanford's Graph-based Neural Dependency Parser at the CoNLL 2017 Shared Task. (2016):20–30.

Dyer, C., Ballesteros, M., Ling, W., Matthews, A., and Smith, N. A. (2015). Transition-Based Dependency Parsing with Stack Long Short-Term Memory. In *Proceedings of the 53rd Annual Meeting of the Association for Computational Linguistics and the 7th International Joint Conference on Natural Language Processing*, pages 334–343, Beijing, China. Association for Computational Linguistics.

Dyer, C., Kuncoro, A., Ballesteros, M., and Smith, N. A. (2016). Recurrent Neural Network Grammars. In *Proc. of NAACL*.

Goldberg, Y. (2017). Neural Network Methods for Natural Language Processing. In *Synthesis Lectures on Human Language Technologies*, volume 10, pages 1–282. Morgan & Claypool Publishers series.

Grave, E., Bojanowski, P., Gupta, P., Joulin, A., and Mikolov, T. (2018). Learning Word Vectors for 157 Languages. In *Proceedings of the International Conference on Language Resources and Evaluation (LREC 2018)*, pages 1–5.

Habash, N. Y. (2010). Introduction to Arabic Natural Language Processing. *Synthesis Lectures on Human Language Technologies*, 3(1):1–187.

Kanerva, J., Ginter, F., Miekka, N., Leino, A., and Salakoski, T. (2018). Turku Neural Parser Pipeline : An End-to-End System for the CoNLL 2018 Shared Task. In *Proceedings of the CoNLL 2018 Shared Task: Multilingual Parsing from Raw Text to Universal Dependencies*, pages 133–142.

Kiperwasser, E. and Goldberg, Y. (2016). Simple and Accurate Dependency Parsing Using Bidirectional LSTM Feature Representations. *Transactions of the Association for Computational Linguistics*, 4:313–327.

Kübler, S., McDonald, R., and Nivre, J. (2009). Dependency Parsing. *Synthesis Lectures on Human Language Technologies*, 34(1):1–127.

Kuncoro, A., Ballesteros, M., Kong, L., Dyer, C., Neubig, G., and Smith, N. A. (2017). What Do Recurrent Neural Network Grammars Learn About Syntax? *arXiv preprint arXiv:1611.05774*.

Lavelli, A. (2016). Comparing State-of-the-art Dependency Parsers on the Italian Stanford Dependency Treebank. *CLiC it*, pages 173–178.

Mcdonald, R., Crammer, K., and Pereira, F. (2005). Online Large-Margin Training of Dependency Parsers. pages 91–98.

Nguyen, D. Q. and Verspoor, K. (2018). An improved neural network model for joint POS tagging and dependency parsing. In *Proceedings of the CoNLL 2018 Shared Task: Multilingual Parsing from Raw Text to Universal Dependencies*, pages 81–91.

Nivre, J. (2008). Algorithms for Deterministic Incremental Dependency Parsing. *Computational Linguistics*, 34(4):513–553.

Nivre, J. (2014). Universal Dependencies for Swedish. In *The Fifth Swedish Language Technology Conference (Sltc)*, pages 1579–1585.

Seyoum, B. E., Miyao, Y., and Mekonnen, B. Y. (2018). Universal Dependencies for Amharic. In Nicoletta Calzolari, et al., editors, *Proceedings of the Eleventh International Conference on Language Resources and Evaluation (LREC 2018)*, pages 2216–2222, Miyazaki, Japan. European Language Resources Association (ELRA).

Smith, A., de Lhoneux, M., Stymne, S., and Nivre, J. (2018). An Investigation of the Interactions Between Pre-Trained Word Embeddings, Character Models and POS Tags in Dependency Parsing. In *Proceedings of the 2018 Conference on Empirical Methods in Natural Language Processing*, pages 2711–2720, Brussels, Belgium. Association for Computational Linguistics.

Straka, M., Hajič, J., and Straková, J. (2016). UDPipe: Trainable Pipeline for Processing CoNLL-U Files Performing Tokenization, Morphological Analysis, POS Tagging and Parsing. In *Proceedings of LREC 2016*, pages 4290–4297.

Straka, M., Straková, J., and Hajič, J. (2017). Prague at EPE 2017: The UDPipe System. In *Proceedings of the 2017 Shared Task on Extrinsic Parser Evaluation at the Fourth International Conference on Dependency Linguistics and the 15th International Conference on Pars-*

ing Technologies, pages 65–74, Pisa (Italy). Association for Computational Linguistics (ACL).

Straková, J., Straka, M., and Hajič, J. (2014). Open-Source Tools for Morphology, Lemmatization, POS Tagging and Named Entity Recognition. In *Proceedings of the 52nd Annual Meeting of the Association for Computational Linguistics: System Demonstrations*, pages 13–18, Baltimore, Maryland USA. Association for Computational Linguistics.

Tsarfaty, R., Seddah, D., Goldberg, Y., Kübler, S., Candito, M., Foster, J., Versley, Y., Rehbein, I., and Tounsi, L. (2010). Statistical parsing of morphologically rich languages (SPMRL): what, how and whither. In *Proceedings of the NAACL HLT 2010 First Workshop on Statistical Parsing of Morphologically-Rich Languages*, pages 1–12, Los Angeles, California. Association for Computational Linguistics.

Zeman, D., Popel, M., Straka, M., Hajic, J., Nivre, J., Ginter, F., Luotolahti, J., Pyysalo, S., Petrov, S., Potthast, M., Tyers, F., Badmaeva, E., Gokirmak, M., Nedoluzhko, A., Cinkova, S., Hajic jr., J., Hlavacova, J., Kettnerová, V., Uresova, Z., Kanerva, J., Ojala, S., Missilä, A., Manning, C. D., Schuster, S., Reddy, S., Taji, D., Habash, N., Leung, H., de Marneffe, M.-C., Sanguinetti, M., Simi, M., Kanayama, H., DePaiva, V., Droganova, K., Martínez Alonso, H., Çöltekin, Ç., Sulubacak, U., Uszkoreit, H., Macketanz, V., Burchardt, A., Harris, K., Marheinecke, K., Rehm, G., Kayadelen, T., Attia, M., Elkahky, A., Yu, Z., Pitler, E., Lertpradit, S., Mandl, M., Kirchner, J., Alcalde, H. F., Strnadová, J., Banerjee, E., Manurung, R., Stella, A., Shimada, A., Kwak, S., Mendonca, G., Lando, T., Nitisaroj, R., and Li, J. (2017). CoNLL 2017 Shared Task: Multilingual Parsing from Raw Text to Universal Dependencies. In *Proceedings of the CoNLL 2017 Shared Task: Multilingual Parsing from Raw Text to Universal Dependencies*, pages 1–19. Association for Computational Linguistics.

Zeman, D., HajiË, J., Popel, M., Potthast, M., Straka, M., Ginter, F., Nivre, J., and Petrov, S. (2018). CoNLL 2018 Shared Task : Multilingual Parsing from Raw Text to Universal Dependencies. In *Proceedings of the CoNLL 2018 Shared Task: Multilingual Parsing from Raw Text to Universal Dependencies*, pages 1–21, Brussels, Belgium. Association for Computational Linguistics.

Zhang, Y. and Nivre, J. (2011). Transition-based Dependency Parsing with Rich Non-local Features. In *Proceedings of the 49th Annual Meeting of the Association for Computational Linguistics: short papers*, pages 188–193. Association for Computational Linguistics.

Proceedings of the First workshop on Resources for African Indigenous Languages (RAIL), pages 31–35
Language Resources and Evaluation Conference (LREC 2020), Marseille, 11–16 May 2020

Mobilizing Metadata: Open Data Kit (ODK) for Language Resource Development in East Africa

Richard T. Griscom
Leiden University
Van Wijkplaats 4, 2311 BX Leiden, Netherlands
r.t.l.griscom@hum.leidenuniv.nl

Abstract

Linguistic fieldworkers collect and archive metadata as part of the language resources (LRs) that they create, but they often work in resource-constrained environments that prevent them from using computers for data entry. In such situations, linguists must complete time-consuming and error-prone digitization tasks that limit the quantity and quality of the resources and metadata that they produce (Thieberger & Berez 2012; Margetts & Margetts 2012). This paper describes a method for entering linguistic metadata into mobile devices using the Open Data Kit (ODK) platform, a suite of open source tools designed for mobile data collection. The method was incorporated into two community-based language documentation projects in Tanzania, involving twelve researchers simultaneously collecting data in four administrative regions (Griscom & Harvey 2019). Through the identification of project-specific data dependencies and redundancies, a number of efficiencies were built into the metadata entry system. These include the use of closed vocabularies, unique data entry forms for distinct data collector categories, and separate forms for entering participant and resource metadata. The resulting system serves as the basis for the ongoing development of general purpose bilingual English-Swahili metadata entry tools, to be made available for use by other researchers working in East Africa.

Keywords: metadata, language resources, Africa

1. Introduction

Collecting linguistic data to support the creation of LRs for indigenous African languages often involves working with communities in areas where regular access to electricity and internet may be limited. These resource restrictions often lead data collectors to utilize paper-based methods that produce non-digital data which must then later be digitized. Digitization is time-consuming and can introduce additional errors to data, so a method that removes digitization from the workflow has distinct advantages (Thieberger & Berez 2012: 92; Margetts & Margetts 2012: 16). The methods and tools described in this paper enable data collectors, working individually or in teams, to create rich digital metadata in remote regions without the need for a computer or internet connection at the time of metadata creation.

1.1 Mobilizing Language Resource Metadata

High quality metadata are crucial for resource discovery (Good 2002), but also for answering research questions that involve extra-linguistic information (Kendall 2008; Kendall 2011). Various metadata standards exist for LRs, including Text Encoding Initiative (TEI), ISLE Meta Data Initiative (IMDI), and Component MetaData Infrastructure (CMDI), among others. There are also multiple linguistic metadata creation tools currently available, such as ProFormA2, Arbil, COMEDI, and CMDI-Maker (Fallucchi, Steffen & De Luca 2019). All metadata creation tools currently available require either a computer or a stable internet connection to function properly.

The need for a new digital metadata entry system that does not rely on a computer or stable internet connection is exacerbated when data collection is on a large scale and conducted by multiple researchers working simultaneously in different regions. These are the exact conditions of two coordinated and community-based language documentation projects in northern Tanzania, funded by the Endangered Languages Documentation Programme (ELDP): "Gorwaa, Hadza, and Ihanzu: Grammatical Inquiries in the Tanzanian Rift" (IFP0285) and "Documenting Hadza: language contact and variation" (IPF0304). Together, these two-year projects involve the participation of 10 local researchers from the Ihanzu and Hadza indigenous communities, distributed across five stations in the Lake Eyasi Basin, as well as two principle investigators (PIs). Figure 1 shows a map of Tanzania with the location of each of the five research stations marked by a dot (Google 2020a).

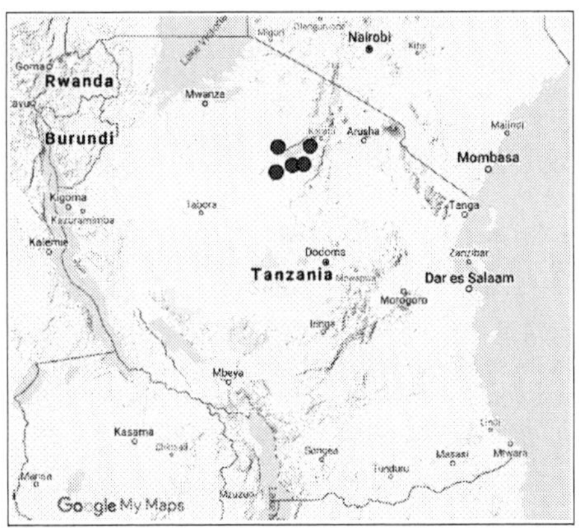

Figure 1: Map of research stations on a national scale

With each of the 12 researchers expected to produce new metadata every week for a period exceeding one calendar year, collecting and digitizing paper-based metadata was not a reasonable option. The majority of data collection for the two projects takes place in areas without electricity or internet, so typical digital metadata creation tools could not be used, either. A new method for mobile metadata entry was needed.

2. Open Data Kit

ODK is a free and open-source software platform for collecting and managing data in resource-constrained environments, and it includes three primary applications of relevance to linguistic metadata collection: ODK Build, a web application for creating custom forms for data entry based on the XForm standard, ODK Aggregate, a Java server application to store, analyze, and export form data, and ODK Collect, an Android application that allows for the entry of data directly into mobile devices. With all three of these components working together, teams of researchers can collect data quickly and simultaneously in remote areas, and all of their data can be compiled together on a single server. Figure 2 shows a schematic of the workflow during data collection: data collectors upload their data to an ODK Aggregate server from their mobile devices, and then a data reviewer compiles the data and exports it from the server for analysis.

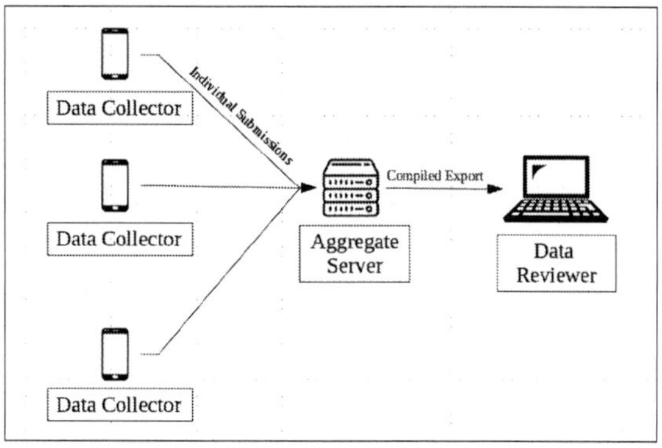

Figure 2: Schematic of the ODK data collection workflow

The following criteria were considered to be crucial for a successful metadata entry system: the removal of digitization from the metadata creation workflow, scalability so that the system could be used by teams of data collectors working independently and simultaneously, the utilization of mobile technology to enable metadata creation in areas without electricity, and an open source software platform that makes the method accessible to the researcher community.

The Open Data Kit (ODK) suite was selected as the primary platform for metadata collection because it satisfies all of the above criteria. It also has additional advantages, including an established record as a data collection platform among NGOs and non-profits working in Africa, support for multilingual data entry forms, and the collection of geo-spatial data.

3. The ODK Linguistic Metadata Method

The ODK metadata entry system created for the Hadza and Ihanzu community language documentation projects was designed and tested over a period of a few months prior to implementation. The method was designed to be as accurate and efficient as possible given the specific needs of the research projects, and later the specifics of the system were used as the basis for the development of general purpose tools.

3.1 Identifying Metadata Needs

A first step in developing a new tool or method is the identification of research values and desiderata (Good 2010). For the language documentation projects in Tanzania, our desiderata were metadata that satisfy the format and content requirements of the Endangered Languages Archive (ELAR), the repository in which project data will be deposited, and metadata that allow for the analysis of language variation and contact, a focus of the research program.

The archive deposits for ELDP projects hosted on ELAR use a metadata profile that includes components for deposit, bundle, resource, and participant metadata (Duin et al. 2019). In total, three deposits were prepared for the two ELDP projects: one for Ihanzu and two for Hadza. A method was thus needed for specifying the appropriate deposit for each bundle. Bundles in ELAR are used to group together different types of resources and participants, so we also needed a method that would facilitate this grouping and correctly categorize resources and participants. The different types of resources include audio and video recordings, as well as text data such as transcriptions and translations. The two categories of participants include researchers and speakers.

The metadata required for studying language variation and contact include resource metadata such as speech genre, interactivity, and location of speech act, as well as participant metadata such as age, gender, education background, location and location history, and language background. Any data entry forms created for the Hadza and Ihanzu projects would therefore need to incorporate fields for entering these types of metadata, and the information would need to be processed in such a way that it can be easily retrieved.

3.2 Creation of Metadata Entry Forms

Once the desired metadata had been identified, metadata entry forms were created using ODK Build. A number of efficiencies were built into the metadata entry system through the identification of project-specific data dependencies and redundancies. These efficiencies included the use of closed vocabularies, unique sets of forms for different categories of data collectors, and the division of resource and participant forms.

3.2.1 Closed Vocabularies and Form Sets

Although many components in the ELAR metadata profile are not restricted to a closed set of possible values, within the context of a research project the value of many components is either constant (e.g. target language, project) or restricted to a closed set (e.g. researcher, equipment used). A metadata creation system tailored to a specific project can therefore incorporate these constants and closed vocabularies to increase speed and accuracy. Rather than create a single metadata entry form for all data collectors, which would include closed vocabulary sets with entries that were not relevant for some data collectors, we created three sets of forms: one set each for principle investigators, Hadza local researchers, and Ihanzu local researchers.

By creating three separate sets of metadata entry forms, we were able to restrict closed sets to only the values that were viable options for each category of data collector. This reduced the likelihood of categorical data entry errors and made the forms easier to navigate with fewer options to choose from.

3.2.2 Session and Speaker Metadata

Speakers often participate in the creation of multiple recordings, but participant metadata is only collected once. For this reason, two separate forms were created for resource metadata and participant metadata. This reduced data redundancy during the data collection stage, but also introduced the requirement for post-collection data processing (see Section 3.4).

3.2.3 Field types and organization

A variety of different entry widgets were integrated into the ODK forms, depending on the type of metadata to be collected. Open text widgets were used for metadata that aren not restricted to closed vocabularies, such as the names of participants and locations. Single choice widgets were used for metadata categories that constitute closed sets of mutually exclusive values, such as the gender of a participant or the name of the researcher collecting data. Multiple choice widgets were used for metadata categories consisting of closed sets of non-mutually exclusive values, such as the languages spoken by a participant. Date widgets were used for metadata such as recording date and participant birth year, a GPS widget was used to retrieve geo-spatial data for the location of recording, and a photo widget was used for creating photos of participants for identification purposes.

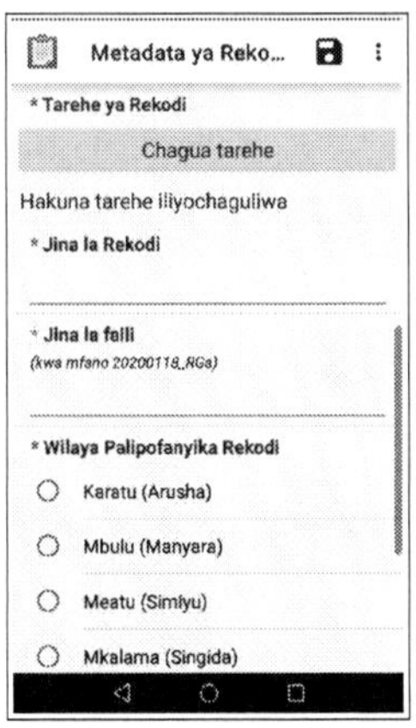

Figure 3: A form for entering recording session metadata

Figure 3 shows a screenshot one of the ODK forms used by local researchers. The "Tarehe ya Rekodi" widget is a date widget used to choose the date of a recording, the "Jina la Rekodi" and "Jina la Faili" widgets are open text widgets for entering the names recordings and files, and the "Wilaya Palipoganyika Rekodi" widget is a single choice widget for choosing the district where a recording was made. The red asterisk by the name of each widget indicates that it is required, and users need to complete these widgets before continuing with the rest of the form.

3.3 Setting up the ODK System

Installation of the mobile device and server components of the ODK system was straightforward and did not require significant technical expertise. An ODK Aggregate server was prepared following the step-by-step directions on the ODK website (ODK 2017) FreeDNS was used to host the server free of cost, and Google Cloud Platform was used to create a virtual server (Google 2020b). Due to the low volume of data, a small virtual server and drive were deemed sufficient (g1-small virtual machine and 30 GB standard persistent disk).

ODK Collect was installed on five Android mobile phones, purchased locally in Tanzania. Each phone was given a unique username that identifies the team using the device to collect metadata. Access information for the ODK Aggregate server was stored in each phone's settings and the appropriate set of metadata entry forms for each phone was downloaded. An administrator password was put in place on each phone so that some options, such as deleting and downloading new forms, were made unavailable to local researchers.

ODK comes pre-installed with support for multiple interface languages. For the local researchers in Tanzania we set the interface to be displayed in Swahili, the lingua franca of East Africa. We additionally designed the forms to be visible in either English or Swahili, and set the default language of the forms as Swahili for the local researcher devices.

Figure 4: Local researchers practice using ODK (Photo credit Nadia Jassim)

During a five-day language documentation training workshop, all local researchers were given instruction on the use of ODK for metadata creation. Local researchers practiced entering data, saving forms, and uploading to the Aggregate server. During the training itself, some minor modifications were made to the forms, including the reordering and rewording of questions, based on feedback from the local researchers.

After the training, and once data collection had been initiated, a few additional modifications were made to the forms. For example, an additional question was added to the recording session metadata forms for the local researchers and PIs to create a unique filename for each recording, which includes the recording date in ISO format (YYYYMMDD), a two-letter code for the researcher who created the recording, and an alphabetic system for organizing the recordings based on the order in which they were created. These filenames are used for all of the resource files associated with a given recording. After local researchers experienced repeated difficulties with data management, it was determined that adding the filename question would make it easier for them to bundle resource files after data collection.

Follow-up visits to research stations provided opportunities to give continued feedback on metadata collection. Common issues included inconsistencies in the spelling of participant names and misunderstandings about meta-linguistic descriptions such as interactivity and speech genre,. The most frequent mistake initially was simply forgetting to enter metadata, either for a resource or a participant.

3.4 Metadata Processing

Through the method described here, metadata is entered into mobile devices and then uploaded to an ODK Aggregate server. The data from that server can then be exported as a comma-separated value (.CSV) file, or streamed live to Google Sheets. All of the submissions for each form can be exported together. In order to produce metadata files in the appropriate format for archiving with ELAR, data from the CSV files for participant and resource metadata forms need to be linked together.

A Python script was created to produce the final metadata files for each bundle to be deposited in ELAR. A bundle is a group of associated resources and participants. The script compiles information from the resource and participant metadata and identifies the types of resource files associated with each recording session to create a bundle that can be deposited in ELAR.

For example, if a given entry in the resource metadata specifies that two speaker-participants were involved in the creation of the recording, then the script uses the participant names in the resource metadata to extract additional metadata for those two speaker-participants from their corresponding entries in the participant metadata, and the script then creates a bundled metadata file using the extracted information.

4. Method Assessment

The competing goals of achieving representative data volume and data accessibility, collectively described by some as the "reproducibility crisis" (Gezelter 2015), can be addressed within the domain of linguistic fieldwork in at least two ways: the active participation of the speech community in data collection ("crowd-sourcing"), and the strategic use of computational technologies ("automation"). The ODK linguistic metadata method attempts to utilize both solutions, and has a number of notable advantages over non-digital entry methods.

The method has the potential to increase the quality, quantity, and consistency of linguistic data and metadata deposited in language archives. It does so not just by reducing processing bottlenecks, which enables linguists to spend more time analyzing or collecting data when they would otherwise be manually digitizing data, but also by opening the door to increased involvement of speech communities in the language documentation process, which has been shown to benefit research outputs by producing linguistic data sets that are more diverse and representative (Czaykowska-Higgins 2009).

The system is not without its limitations, however. As with any metadata entry system, open text fields will still contain errors that must be checked either manually or through an automated system of some kind. Additional training and feedback may reduce the error rate, but it is not reasonable to expect error-free metadata with any system that utilizes open text fields.

The submissions for updated versions of forms need to be manually compiled together with the submissions for previous versions, at least in the current version of the ODK Aggregate software. The significance of this task depends on the volume and timing of updates made to forms. If forms are submitted through ODK Collect using a previous version that has since been deleted from the device, then those forms can no longer be viewed locally on the device. Again, the significance of this limitation depends on the volume and timing of updates.

Perhaps the biggest limitation, however, is that the output of the ODK suite must be formatted according to the metadata profile of the corresponding language archive. This requires some coding and therefore restricts the pool of researchers capable of designing a project-specific implementation to those with coding knowledge or access to someone with that knowledge.

5. Towards a Standardized System

One way to decrease the learning curve for the ODK metadata system is to develop a set of standardized general purpose forms, based on one or more common metadata profiles, and an accompanying processing script. The Hadza and Ihanzu community language documentation projects in Tanzania are now serving as the foundation for the creation of such a set of tools. Initially, these tools will be based on the ELAR metadata profile and restricted to English and Swahili interfaces, which should be useful for researchers working with endangered language communities in East Africa. In the future, it is planned to expand the tools to include a French interface and metadata profiles for other common language archives and data repositories.

6. Conclusion

The piloted ODK linguistic metadata system offers a number of advantages when compared to manual data entry methods. The removal of digitization and the use of closed-vocabularies increase the accuracy and speed of metadata entry. This is significant because it allows for the creation of large and representative datasets, which are a primary goal of language documentation (Himmelmann 1998; Himmelmann 2006; Woodbury 2003). The scalability of the ODK system also allows teams of data collectors to work together, which can allow for increased community engagement and collaboration.

The system specifically developed for the Hadza and Ihanzu community language documentation projects relies on project-specific and repository-specific closed vocabularies and constant values, but these specificities inform the design of general purpose metadata entry tools. It is hoped that these tools will make the possibility of digital metadata creation a reality for researchers working throughout remote regions of Africa.

Acknowledgements

The research reported in this paper is supported by the Endangered Languages Documentation Programme (ELDP, IPF0304) and the Leiden University Centre for Digital Humanities (LUCDH).

7. Bibliographical References

Czaykowska-Higgins, Ewa. 2009. Research Models, Community Engagement, and Linguistic Fieldwork: Reflections on Working within Canadian Indigenous Communities. Language Documentation and Conservation 3(1). 15–50.

Duin, Patrick, Twan Goosen, Mitchell Seaton, Olha Shkaravska, George Georgovassilis & Jean-Charles Ferrieres. 2019. CMDI Component Registry. CLARIN. https://catalog.clarin.eu/ds/ComponentRegistry/#/.

Fallucchi, Francesca, Hennicke Steffen & Ernesto William De Luca. 2019. Creating CMDI-Profiles for Textbook Resources. In Emmanouel Garoufallou, Fabio Sartori, Rania Siatri & Marios Zervas (eds.), Metadata and Semantic Research, vol. 846, 302–314. Cham: Springer International Publishing. doi:10.1007/978-3-030-14401-2_28. http://link.springer.com/10.1007/978-3-030-14401-2_28 (13 February, 2020).

Gezelter, Daniel J. 2015. Open Source and Open Data Should Be Standard Practices. The journal of physical chemistry letters 6(7). 1168–1169.

Good, Jeff. 2002. A Gentle Introduction to Metadata. http://www.language-archives.org/documents/gentle-intro.html.

Good, Jeff. 2010. Valuing technology: Finding the linguist's place in a new technological universe. Language Documentation, Practice and values. Amsterdam: John Benjamins.

Google. 2020. Google Cloud Platform. https://cloud.google.com.

Griscom, Richard T. & Andrew Harvey. 2019. Gorwaa, Hadza, and Ihanzu: Language contact, variation, and grammatical inquiries in the Tanzanian Rift. Presented at the East Africa Day Leiden, Leiden. https://doi.org/10.5281/zenodo.3509475.

Himmelmann, Nikolaus P. 1998. Documentary and descriptive linguistics. Linguistics 36. 161–195.

Himmelmann, Nikolaus P. 2006. Language documentation: What is it and what is it good for? In Jost Gippert, Nikolaus P. Himmelmann & Ulrike Mosel (eds.), Essentials of Language Documentation. Berlin: Mouton de Gruyter.

Kendall, Tyler. 2008. On the History and Future of Sociolinguistic Data. Language and Linguistics Compass 2(2). 332–351. doi:10.1111/j.1749-818X.2008.00051.x.

Kendall, Tyler. 2011. Corpora from a sociolinguistic perspective. Revista Brasileira de Linguística Aplicada 11(2). 361–389. doi:10.1590/S1984-63982011000200005.

Margetts, Anna & Andrew Margetts. 2012. Audio and video recording techniques for linguistic research. The Oxford Handbook of Linguistic Fieldwork. Oxford University Press.

ODK. 2017. Getting Started With ODK. https://docs.opendatakit.org/getting-started/#install-aggregate-optional.

Thieberger, Nicholas & Andrea L. Berez. 2012. Linguistic Data Management. The Oxford Handbook of Linguistic Fieldwork. Oxford University Press.

Woodbury, Anthony C. 2003. Defining Documentary Linguistics. Language Documentation and Description, vol. 1. London: Hans Rausing Endangered Languages Project.

Proceedings of the First workshop on Resources for African Indigenous Languages (RAIL), pages 36–44
Language Resources and Evaluation Conference (LREC 2020), Marseille, 11–16 May 2020

A computational grammar of Ga

Lars Hellan
Norwegian University of Science and Technology, Norway
lars.hellan@ntnu.no

Abstract
The paper describes aspects of an HPSG style computational grammar of the West African language Ga (a Kwa language spoken in the Accra area of Ghana). As a Volta Basin Kwa language, Ga features many types of multiverb expressions and other particular constructional patterns in the verbal and nominal domain. The paper highlights theoretical and formal features of the grammar motivated by these phenomena, some of them possibly innovative to the formal framework. As a so-called deep grammar of the language, it hosts a rich lexical structure, and we describe ways in which the grammar builds on previously available lexical resources. We outline an environment of current resources in which the grammar is part, and lines of research and development in which it and its environment can be used.

Keywords: Ga, Kwa, computational grammar, typed feature structures, construction level compositional analysis, nominal structures, multiverb constructions

1. Introduction[1]

Ga is a Kwa language spoken in the Accra area of Ghana with about 745,000 speakers[2]. Linguistic descriptions date back to early 1800 (cf. Rask (1828)), and although digital text resources are few, it is well studied linguistically, and has some advanced resources such as the Ga-English dictionary (Dakubu 2009). The present article describes digital resources which in important respects derive from this dictionary and its underlying Toolbox lexicon. We mainly focus on a computational grammar of Ga, whose development started in 2005, and also on a valence lexicon, whose development started in 2008. The developments were coordinated, althought each at its own pace, and conducted jointly by Professor Mary Esther Kropp Dakubu and the author until Prof. Dakubu's death in 2016.

Computational grammars are programs which automatically assign various types of analysis to sentences of a language – they range from morphological parsers, which recognize words' part of speech (POS) and morphological build-up, via dependency parsers which recognize syntactic phrases and dependency relations between words internal to a phrase and between phrases, to so-called 'deep' parsers which also recognize lexical structures and semantic properties of words and their combinations. Deep parsers reflect frameworks of formal grammar such as Lexical Functional Grammar (abbreviated 'LFG', cf. Bresnan (2001)) and Head-Driven Phrase structure grammar (abbreviated 'HPSG', cf. Pollard and Sag (1994), Copestake (2002)); the grammar to be presented mainly follows HPSG but with some elements of LFG; it technically is developed at the LKB platform described in Copestake (2002).

Verb valence lexicons are lexicons giving concise enumerations of the valence frames of each verb, i.e., enumerations of the possible environments of a verb described in terms of the so-called *valence-bound* items in the environments (following the terminology of Tesnière (1959)). A principled meeting point between valence lexicons and deep grammars is that the verb lexicon of a deep grammar will have explicit valence information. From either side one can thereby derive the other (and even in turn perform cyclical improvements, taking advantage of articulations on the derived side proving useful also on the other side, and vice versa). In the present case, once the valence lexicon was established, it was imported into the grammar.

Both types of resources have a solid foundation in Indo-European languages, and one can name various kinds of practical applications that they serve. However, equally interesting is what these resources for Ga can tell us regarding what are basic and necessary structures of grammar and valence. For instance, in an HPSG based grammar, the distinction between *argument* (i.e., valence-bound) and *adjunct* (i.e., not valence-bound) is basic like in linguistic traditions in Indo-European languages, and a question is whether it can be maintained in a grammar of a Kwa language. Likewise, the grammatical articulation of some semantic structures is quite different in Ga from what one expects in Indo-European languages.

To be more concrete, Kwa languages like Ga and Akan are known to make little use of prepositions and adjectives, so that constructions involving nouns and verbs may be seen as playing a larger role than, e.g., in Indo-European languages. Thus *multiverb expressions* are known to play a large role in the languages, subsuming *Serial Verb Constructions (SVCs)*, *Extended Verb Complexes (EVCs)* which are sequences of preverbs preceding a main verb, and *Verbid Constructions (ViD)*, where verb phrases play a role similar to what adverbials play in Indo-European languages (see Dakubu 2004a, 2008, Dakubu et al. 2007, Dakubu 2013 for analysis of many of the construction types). Such constructions raise the question whether there can be more than one verbal head per sentence; and if not, whether the argument-adjunct distinction is at all relevant to describing the relationships between the verbs. A further reflex of the lack of prepositions is that spatial specification often take the shape of transitive constructions. Moreover, pre-nominal specifiers manifest a complexity well beyond what one finds in Indo-European languages. The latter construction types will be exemplified and analyzed in section 2. In section 3 we exemplify and show the analysis of multiverb constructions. Section 4 recapitulates the development of the valence lexicon from the Toolbox

[1] I am grateful to the three reviewers for helpful comments.
[2] ISO-639-3 «gaa». Number of speakers in 2013.
https://www.ethnologue.com/country/GH/languages

source, and accompanying resources. Section 5 discusses possible further developments of the resources described. Examples throughout are from the works by Dakubu cited above, from the 'Ga Appendix' to Hellan and Dakubu 2010, and from Dakubu (Unpublished a). The latter is the presentation of the valence lexicon that we will be referring to, with about 2000 entries, where each entry represents *one* frame of a given verb. Thus, when a verb has *n* frames, it will be represented in *n* entries. To each entry is provided a short example, whereby this is also a corpus of short sentences.

2. Nominal complexes with relational nouns and possessive constructions

2.1 Examples

Nominal complexes with relational nouns and possessive constructions are exemplified in (1):

(1)

a.

v Ee-la	e-daa-ŋ
3S.PROG-sing	3S.POSS-mouth-LOC"
V	N

"He's murmuring incoherently to himself."
(literally: 'he is singing his mouth')

b.

E-ŋmra	e-toi-ŋ
3S.AOR-scrape	3S.POSS-ear-LOC
V	N

"She slapped him."
(literally: 'she scraped his ear')

c.

E-tsuinaa	mii-funta	lɛ
3S.POSS-desire	PROG-nauseate	3S
N	V	PN

"She feels sick, nauseous."
(literally: 'her desire nauseates her')

d.

Mi-yitso	mii-gba	mi
1S.POSS-head	PROG-split	1S
N	V	PN

"My head is aching."
(literally: 'my head splits me')

e.

O-he	jɔ-ɔ	bo
2S.POSS-self	cool-HAB	2S
N	V	PN

"you are at ease."
(literally: 'your self cools you')

In each sentence, the full NP is headed by a relational noun which has a possessive specifier, and this specifier is coreferential with a pronoun (as prefix or freestanding). Of the 2000 sentences in the corpus mentioned, no less than 690 have an object headed by a relational noun, and 100 have a subject headed by a relational noun, often with a bodypart or identity reading. This attests to the importance of analytically representing nominal complexes with relational nouns and possessive constructions.

2.2 Analysis

A first installment of the grammar follows the HPSG Matrix (Bender et al. 2010), illustrated in Dakubu et al. 2007, while in a more recent version the grammar is designed according to the architecture outlined in Hellan 2019; both use the LKB platform, whose formalism is a Typed Feature Structure (TFS) system. Information in such a system is generally exposed through Attribute Value Matrices (AVMs), where each AVM belongs to a *type*, and attributes are introduced (declared) according to the following conventions:

[A] A given type introduces the same attribute(s) no matter in which environment it is used.

[B] A given attribute is declared by one type only (but occurs with all of its subtypes).

In a TFS representing a grammar, there are many type hierarchies, representing POS, tenses, semantic roles, etc.; some of these hierarchies do without attributes, while the following ones do. Types for grammatical functions (values of the attribute 'GF') and actants (participants in semantic argument structure, represented as values of the attribute 'ACTNT') include those indicated below: the *gramfct* subtypes declare the GF attributes ('SUBJ' and 'OBJ') and the *actnt* subtypes declare the semantic argument structure attributes ('ACT1' and 'ACT2'):

```
(2) a.   gramfct                  b.        actnt
          /      \                          /       \
     su-gf        ob-gf           act1-rel          act2-rel
[SUBJ sign]  [OBJ sign]         [ACT1index]       [ACT2 index]
          \      /                          \       /
        su-ob-gf                           act12-rel
```

The way in which these attributes combine in an AVM of a transitive structure, as in a sentence like *John ate the cake*, is illustrated in (3); the co-numbering '1' and '2' indicate that the referential index of the subject is the ACT(ant)1 and the referential index of the object is the ACT(ant)2:

(3)

$$\begin{bmatrix} \text{HEAD verb} \\ \text{GF} \begin{bmatrix} \text{SUBJ} \left[\text{INDX } \boxed{1} [\text{ROLE agent}]\right] \\ \text{OBJ} \left[\text{INDX } \boxed{2} [\text{ROLE aff-increm}]\right] \end{bmatrix} \\ \text{ASPECT completed} \\ \text{ACTNT} \begin{bmatrix} \text{ACT1 } \boxed{1} \\ \text{ACT2 } \boxed{2} \end{bmatrix} \end{bmatrix}$$

While a structure like (3) will reflect constructional features of a sentence like *John ate the cake*, a representation of what it *means* will also reflect the content of the various words. A strategy of 'first stepping stone semantics' is to simply put in a representation of the word itself in a slot designated for semantic argument structure, which for the sentence in question will mean extending (3) as (4) (modulo definiteness marking of the object):

(4)

$$\begin{bmatrix} \text{HEAD verb} \\ \text{GF} \begin{bmatrix} \text{SUBJ} \begin{bmatrix} \text{INDX } \boxed{1}[\text{ROLE agent}] \\ \text{ACTNT } [\text{PRED } \textit{John}] \end{bmatrix} \\ \text{OBJ} \begin{bmatrix} \text{INDX } \boxed{2}[\text{ROLE aff-increm}] \\ \text{ACTNT } [\text{PRED } \textit{cake} - \textit{rel}] \end{bmatrix} \end{bmatrix} \\ \text{ASPECT completed} \\ \text{ACTNT} \begin{bmatrix} \text{PRED } \textit{eat - rel} \\ \text{ACT1 } \boxed{1} \\ \text{ACT2 } \boxed{2} \end{bmatrix} \end{bmatrix}$$

To obtain this, each word must be lexically specified for its semantic contribution, along with a recipe of how it fits in relative to the overall structure (4). The use of *valence lists* in HPSG serves such a purpose; for the case in point, eat will thereby have as its lexical specification a structure like (5), where the valence list attributes SPR and COMPS enumerate the items with which the word has to combine (where failure for appropriate items to obtain in the word string to be analyzed means that this lexical structure is not appropriate for the analysis process):[3]

(5)

$$\begin{bmatrix} \text{HEAD verb} \\ \text{ORTH "eat"} \\ \text{GF} \begin{bmatrix} \text{SUBJ } \boxed{1}\big[\text{INDX } \boxed{3}[\text{ROLE agent}]\big] \\ \text{OBJ } \boxed{2}\big[\text{INDX } \boxed{4}[\text{ROLE aff-increm}]\big] \end{bmatrix} \\ \text{SPR } \langle \boxed{1} \rangle \\ \text{COMPS } \langle \boxed{2} \rangle \\ \text{ACTNT} \begin{bmatrix} \text{PRED } \textit{eat - rel} \\ \text{ACT1 } \boxed{3} \\ \text{ACT2 } \boxed{4} \end{bmatrix} \end{bmatrix}$$

A parsing algorithm is in principle necessary if one wants to construe a grammar as *compositional*, since compositionality resides in combinatorial relations between constituents, meaning that a grammar as a whole is compositional if all phenomena to be covered by it can be construed exclusively in terms of combinatorial operations involving all parts of the sentences analysed.

It may be noted that standard HPSG in this respect is a parsing approach exclusively, in that it does not include GF notions, so that a parse representation will be without GF and with both valence lists empty, thus being less informative than (4). Adding such notions to the parsing formalism strengthens the formalism, which might be unwanted on other grounds, yielding a situation where one chooses between formats on other grounds than plainly empirical. However, as we turn to the selected areas of Ga grammar to be considered, we will see that even from parsing perspectives, there may be reasons to use GF in the formalism. In (1d), repeated:

(1d)

Mi-yitso	mii-gba	mi
1S.POSS-head	PROG-split	1S
N	V	PN

"My head is aching."
(literally: my head splits me')

we want to represent the subject as a possessive phrase, where the referent of the whole phrase is a (body)part of the specifier 'mi', and this specifier is also identical to the object; in terms of semantics. The first of these constellations we may represent as in (6), labeled as 'subject is a BodyPart of subject's specifier' (of course speaking of their referents), and the second as (7), in a similar vein labeled as 'subject's specifier is Identical to object':

(6)

$$\textit{suBPsuSpec} \begin{bmatrix} \text{GF} \begin{bmatrix} \text{SUBJ} \begin{bmatrix} \text{INDX } \boxed{1} \\ \text{GF}\big[\text{SPEC}\big[\text{INDX } \boxed{2}\big]\big] \\ \text{ACTNT} \begin{bmatrix} \text{PRED 'is-bodypart-of'-rel} \\ \text{ACT1 } \boxed{1} \\ \text{ACT2 } \boxed{2} \end{bmatrix} \end{bmatrix} \end{bmatrix} \end{bmatrix}$$

(7)

$$\textit{suSpecIDob} \begin{bmatrix} \text{GF} \begin{bmatrix} \text{SUBJ } \big[\text{GF}\big[\text{SPEC}\big[\text{INDX } \boxed{2}\big]\big]\big] \\ \text{OBJ } \big[\text{INDX } \boxed{2}\big] \end{bmatrix} \end{bmatrix}$$

In a full representation of the sentence, (6) and (7) should unify with the verb representation as (8):

(8)

$$\begin{bmatrix} \text{GF} \begin{bmatrix} \text{SUBJ} \begin{bmatrix} \text{INDX } \boxed{1} \\ \text{GF}\big[\text{SPEC}\big[\text{INDX } \boxed{2}\big]\big] \\ \text{ACTNT} \begin{bmatrix} \text{PRED 'is-bodypart-of'-rel} \\ \text{ACT1 } \boxed{1} \\ \text{ACT2 } \boxed{2} \end{bmatrix} \end{bmatrix} \\ \text{OBJ } [\text{INDX 2}] \end{bmatrix} \\ \text{ACTNT} \begin{bmatrix} \text{PRED 'gba'-rel} \\ \text{ACT1 } \boxed{1} \\ \text{ACT2 } \boxed{2} \end{bmatrix} \end{bmatrix}$$

However, although *gba* 'split' is a transitive verb, defining it simply on the model of (5) will fail to induce the relations between the specifier of the subject and the subject and object. What is needed is a lexical representation able to 'look down' into the subject, thus 'seeing' the item that relative to a valence list of the head noun would be representable as the list '<[SPR]>'. This represents a pattern of 'non-locality' for which the valence list notation is not defined (i.e., meaning specifying a list inside of an item inside the 'SPR' list). A way in which we avoid violating this restriction is by, instead of an extra embedded list, using GF attributes reflecting the way they are used in (8), so that the lexical

[3] See Hellan (2019a) for details on introduction of lexical types.

specification for gba relative to the kind of frame in question is (9):

(9) Lexical entry of *gba* in (1d):

$$
\begin{bmatrix}
\text{GF} & \begin{bmatrix}
\text{SUBJ [3]} & \begin{bmatrix}
\text{INDX } \boxed{1} \\
\text{GF}\begin{bmatrix}\text{SPEC}\begin{bmatrix}\text{INDX } \boxed{2}\end{bmatrix}\end{bmatrix} \\
\text{ACTNT} \begin{bmatrix}\text{PRED 'is-bodypart-of'-rel} \\ \text{ACT1 } \boxed{1} \\ \text{ACT2 } \boxed{2}\end{bmatrix}
\end{bmatrix} \\
\text{OBJ [4]} & \begin{bmatrix}\text{INDX } \boxed{2}\end{bmatrix}
\end{bmatrix} \\
\text{SPR} & \langle \boxed{3} \rangle \\
\text{COMPS} & \langle \boxed{4} \rangle \\
\text{ACTNT} & \begin{bmatrix}\text{PRED 'split'-rel} \\ \text{ACT1 } \boxed{1} \\ \text{ACT2 } \boxed{2}\end{bmatrix}
\end{bmatrix}
$$

With similar reasoning for the other cases in (1) and related constructions, this demonstrates the use of including GFs as a construct also in the parsing algorithm. Similar cases have not been prominent in the discussion of the design of standard version of HPSG, and so the phenomenon of Nominal complexes with relational nouns and possessive constructions may represent motivation for this item of modification of the general formal design, and thus a motivation coming from Ga. It has been adopted in the current grammar.

3. Multiverb expressions

Multiverb expressions types are well exemplified in the literature,[4] so here we just point to two types and discuss some aspects of their analysis.

3.1 Serial Verb Construction (SVC)

An SVC appears as a sequencing of any number of VPs, with pervasive uniformity between the verbs, both in their morphology and regarding their arguments. Interpretations range from temporal sequences of events reflecting the sequencing of VPs to pairwise more special combinations. (10) is an example of the latter (from Dakubu (unpublished a)):

(10)	Á-gbele	gbɛ	á-ha	bo
	3.PRF-open	road	3.PRF-give	2S
	V	N	V	Pron

'You have been granted permission.'

This SVC has two verbs, and as is often the case in Ga SVCs, both with the subject expressed by a clitic; the subjects are identical, and likewise the aspects of the verbs.

In AVM form, this can be provisionally exposed as follows, where the notions 'V1', 'V2' are standard labels for the VPs in an SVC sequence:

(11)

$$
\begin{bmatrix}
\text{V1} & \begin{bmatrix}
\text{HEAD } \textit{verb} \\
\text{GF} \begin{bmatrix}\text{SUBJ}\begin{bmatrix}\text{INDX } \boxed{1}\end{bmatrix} \\ \text{OBJ}\begin{bmatrix}\text{INDX } \boxed{2}\end{bmatrix}\end{bmatrix} \\
\text{ACTNT} \begin{bmatrix}\text{PRED } \textit{open-rel} \\ \text{ACT1 } \boxed{1} \\ \text{ACT2 } \boxed{2} \\ \text{ASPECT } \boxed{4}\ \textit{perf}\end{bmatrix}
\end{bmatrix} \\
\text{V2} & \begin{bmatrix}
\text{HEAD } \textit{verb} \\
\text{GF} \begin{bmatrix}\text{SUBJ}\begin{bmatrix}\text{INDX } \boxed{1}\end{bmatrix} \\ \text{OBJ}\begin{bmatrix}\text{INDX } \boxed{3}\end{bmatrix}\end{bmatrix} \\
\text{ACTNT} \begin{bmatrix}\text{PRED } \textit{give-rel} \\ \text{ACT1 } \boxed{1} \\ \text{ACT2 } \boxed{3} \\ \text{ASPECT } \boxed{4}\end{bmatrix}
\end{bmatrix}
\end{bmatrix}
$$

We now face the question whether the SVC should be counted as multi-headed, or whether there are linguistic reasons to count one VP as head and the other as something else. VPs in SVCs are generally too tightly integrated to count as coordination structures – cf. Hellan et al. (2003) for a discussion relative to temporally sequenced VPs in SVCs in Akan (commonly referred to as 'chaining SVCs), an argumentation which may well also hold for Ga, and especially for a case like this where the interpretation is not one of temporal sequencing. If not a coordination structure, another possibility may be a structure of complementation: although *gbele* ('open') does not have a meaning which would motivate counting the subsequent VP as a complement, one might perhaps count the whole construction as a phraseological unit and technically count the first verb as binding the second VP to it as a fixed part. The third option is an analysis of the sequencing of VPs is as *adjunction* between the VPs; this is in general plausible for cases of temporally sequenced VPs where any number of VPs can freely occur; structures like (10) could then be treated as a limiting case of such structures.

Given this as most plausible for the 'free' VP sequences, how can this be formally implemented, and how would the attributes V1 and V2 in case be introduced? Adjunction to, or modification of, VPs is commonly construed as the adjunct being a predicate of the event expressed by the head VP. This will be false for the VP sequencing, since the adjoined VP is predicated of the same entity as the head VP is predicated of. To express this, the grammar must contain, in addition to the 'event modification' rule, a modification rule imposing coreference between the subjects. (12) is such a rule, equating the ACT1 of the adjunct ('NON-HEAD-DTR') not to the event index of the head, but to the index of its

[4] For a recent overview concerning Akan and Ga, see Beermann and Hellan (2018).

subject; we here also indicate the introduction of 'V1' and 'V2'[5].

(12) *Head-Modifier rule II* (partial formlation)

$$\begin{bmatrix} \text{INDX } \boxed{2} \\ \text{HEAD-DTR } \boxed{4} \begin{bmatrix} \text{GF} \left[\text{SUBJ} \left[\text{INDX } \boxed{3}\right]\right] \\ \text{COMPS} \langle\,\rangle \\ \text{INDX } \boxed{2} \end{bmatrix} \\ \text{NONHEAD-DTR } \boxed{5} \begin{bmatrix} \text{MOD} \left\langle \boxed{4} \left[\text{INDX } \boxed{3}\right] \right\rangle \\ \text{COMPS} \langle\,\rangle \\ \text{ACTNT} \left[\text{ACT1 } \boxed{3}\right] \end{bmatrix} \\ \text{V1 } \boxed{4} \\ \text{V2 } \boxed{5} \end{bmatrix}$$

This rule schema will apply recursively when there are more than two VPs.

The motivated status of such a rule of modification is again a respect in which Ga and similar languages may be seen as adding a formal possibility to the formal inventories sustained so far.[6]

The by far most common pattern of 'argument sharing' in SVCs is one of identical subjects. In the literature also identity between objects has been recognized – as 'object sharing' – and even identity between the object of one VP and the subject of the following VP, called 'switch sharing'. These are rare in Ga, but exemplified in Akan by examples like (13):[7]

(13)
'*switch* sharing' between object of one verb and subject of the subsequent verb (Akan)

Kofi	to-o	ne	nan	wɔ-ɔ	Kwame
Kofi	throw-PRF	3Poss	leg	pierce-PRF	Kwame
N	V	Pron	N	V	N

'Kofi kicked Kwame'

Unlike the case above, where both COMPS lists are empty at the point where two VPs combine, one here needs to be able to state that the object of the first VP is identical to the ACT1 of the second VP. Such an identity is hard to state if all one can refer to in the first VP is an empty COMPS list. Once the object is also represented in the GF specification of the first VP, however, one has a reference point.[8] An example with object sharing in Ga is given in (16) below. Although the status of both of these patterns involving objects is a bit controversial, both construction types are accommodated in the grammar, and may potentially provide further motivation for including GF notions in the grammar formalism.

3.2 Extended Verb Complex (EVC) and more

For descriptions of this construction in Ga see Dakubu (2008), Dakubu et al. (2007), Dakubu (2004a), and in Dangme, see Dakubu (1987). The construction type holds a particular interest in that EVCs act as single verbs relative to the environment, but are dividable into word-like units, namely a limited number of *preverbs* (up to three in a row) together with the *main verb*. A simple example is the Ga sentence (14), where *kɛ* is a preverb:

(14)

Tɛte	kɛ-ba-biɛ
Tettey	take-come-here
N	V

"Tettey brought it here."

The valence of the main verb determines the valence of the whole relative to the containing clause, its subject is necessarily the subject of all the preverbs with the same role, and its Aspect, Modality and Polarity marking is wholly determined from left to right. Most preverbs are intransitive, only *kɛ* is transitive.

EVCs, which are perhaps themselves frozen SVCs, can serve in the role of verbs also in SVCs, which gives a complex structure of verb embeddings. Unlike SVCs, in EVCs a complementation analysis is reasonable, since a preverb needs to be followed by a verb – another preverb, or the main verb. These analyses are laid out in Dakubu et al. (2007) and Hellan and Dakubu (2010), and included in the grammar formalism.

Also to be mentioned is the construction in (15):

(15) E-ba tsu mli
3S-AOR-come room inside
"he entered the room ."

The phrase *tsu mli* in our resources is counted as a noun phrase, and acting as object of *ba* ('come', which in addition has intransitive and other uses).[9]

4. Developing the resources

The backbone of a deep computational grammar is its lexicon. The starting point for this lexicon in the Ga grammar is a Toolbox project holding data of the general-purpose published dictionary (Dakubu 2009). The lexicon file in this project consists of 80,000 lines of code, with 7080 entries, of which 5014 for nouns, and 935 for verbs, of which 722 were annotated for valence. From this

[5] By convention, in the constellation (i), the path 'V2.V2' can be read as 'V3', and similarly for higher numbers of VPs.

(i)

$$\begin{bmatrix} \text{V1} \\ \text{V2} \begin{bmatrix} \text{V1} \\ \text{V2} \end{bmatrix} \end{bmatrix}$$

[6] The schema will also be relevant in Indic and other languages with so-called co(n)-verb constructions, where the syntax by itself is marked as modification – and thus unlike the Volta Basin SVC pattern – whereas the argument identities which can obtain match the present case.

[7] Presented by Clement Appah at a seminar in Legon, Ghana.

[8] See Hellan 2019 for details.

[9] Cf. Beermann and Hellan (to appear). In the lexical resource addressed in section 4, this use of *ba* has the code 'ba_3 : v-tr-obPostp-suAg_obLoc-MOTIONDIRECTED'.

Toolbox repository a valence lexicon was created. As a first step the Toolbox lexicon was augmented by valence information such that each entry reflects a unique valence frame or multiverb environment. For instance, for the verb *su* as used in the sentence (16),

(16) E-su lɛ e-gbe lɛ
3S.AOR-bewitch 3S 3S.AOR-kill 3S
'she killed him by magic'

the design of a lexical entry in the amended Toolbox version is as shown in Figure 1; the valence codes are written into the lexical entry following the general 'field' style of Toolbox, where the fields marked \pdl-\pdv represent inflectional information of the lexeme, and the fields \xe, \xg, \xv together constitute a standard linguistic glossing with \xv as a word-and-morph break-up, \xg as morphological and English gloss, and \xe as a free English translation; the valence (or, as here, SVC environment) is encoded as the fields starting with \sl…;.[10]

```
\lx su
\hm 3
\ph su˷`
\ps verb annotated
\sn 1
\de poison
\sn 2
\ge bewitch
\de bewitch, practice black magic, kill by
magic
\sl1 svSuAspIDALL_suAg-
\sl2 v1tr-
\sl3 v1obIDv2ob-
\sl4 obTrgt-
\sl2 v2tr-
\sl4 v2obTh-
\sl5 CAUSATIONwithCAUSINGEVENT-
\sl6 CHANGEofSTATE
\xv E-su lɛ e-gbe lɛ
\xg 3S.AOR-bewitch 3S 3S.AOR-kill 3S
\xe she killed him by magic.
\pdl v. iter
\pdv susui
\pdl n. ag
\pdv sulɔ
\pdl n. ger
\pdv suu
\dt 15/Jan/2010
```

Figure 1 Example of Ga Toolbox entry enriched with CL valence/construction annotation

A verb with more than one valence frame having one entry specified per frame, the verb *ba*, for instance, is represented by 15 different entries in this edition of the Toolbox file. 547 verb lexemes here received altogether 2006 entries annotated in this fashion. In Figure 1, the specification '\hm 3' indicates that this is the third entry with the form *su*.

The code specifications in the \sl-fields are pulled together in a single string as in (17) (omitting \sl15 and \sl16)[11], read as 'a SVC where subject and aspect are identical in all VPs, the role of subject is agent, the head of the second VP is transitive, the first VP's object is identical to the second VPs object, and the object in the second VP is theme':[12]

(17) svSuAspIDALL_suAg-v2tr-v1obIDv2ob-v2obTh

Labels in this style were independently developed as the system *Construction Labeling* formalism (CL) (cf. Hellan and Dakubu 2010, Dakubu and Hellan 2016), and one of the languages to which it was applied was Ga, in a construction type inventory given in Hellan and Dakubu 2010.

The verb part of the lexical resource was turned into a lexical data structure of the type used in HPSG grammars, consisting of 1980 sequentially numbered entries, with the CL specification indicating the *lexical/construction type* to which the entry belongs.[13] Figure 2 is the direct counterpart to the Toolbox entry in Figure 1, with *su_1448* as the entry identifier, and the formula part

':= …'

meaning 'belongs to the construction type '… '; this information is stated relative to the first verb, which is thus, formally, counted as a head:

```
su_1448 := svSuAspIDALL_suAg-v2tr-v1obIDv2ob-v2obTh &
 [STEM <"su">,
 PHON <"su">,
 ENGL-GLOSS <"bewitch">,
 EXAMPLE "E-su lɛ e-gbe lɛ",
 GLOSS "3S.AOR-bewitch 3S 3S.AOR-kill 3S",
 FREE-TRANSL "she killed him by magic."].
```

Figure 2 Grammar style counterpart to entry in Figure 1

While this is a constructional representation, a valence representation can be derived in a similar manner from a Toolbox entry, thus, the entry in Figure 3 will directly go into the grammar lexicon as a valence entry of type 'transitive with agentive subject and theme object':

[10] With such IGTs illustrating verbs and smaller phrases illustrating nouns and other POS, these specifications in the Toolbox file constitute a large corpus which however yet remains to be implemented on a standard corpus format; this situation may apply to Toolbox files for other languages as well.

[11] This is a *Situation Type* label, an aspect of analysis not so far fully integrated in the grammar; as an annotation resource, cf. Hellan (2020). It's a common observation that many SVCs express a 'unique situation', thus that the verb meanings do not constitute separate events but are merged into a single event. Hellan (2019b) is an attempt to give formal expression to this notion, in terms of a layer of semantic representation called *Situation Structure*, whose interaction with *Semantic Argument Structure* is outlined in Hellan (2019a), and whose encoding in *Situation Type labels* is outlined Hellan (2020).

[12] The identity of the objects is here not included in the 'IDALL' part, leaving open if it is a matter of argument sharing rather than pronominal coreference. Since Ga often realizes subject sharing through pronominal pro-clitics, a counterpart to this strategy for objects could be conceived.

[13] Conducted by Tore Bruland; also cf. Hirzel 2006.

```
fee_244 := v-tr-suAg_obTh &
 [STEM <"fee">,
 PHON <"fee">,
 ENGL-GLOSS <"make">,
 EXAMPLE "E-fee flɔɔ, samala",
 GLOSS "3S.AOR-make stew, soap",
 FREE-TRANSL "she made stew, soap."].
```

Figure 3 Ga Grammar style valence entry

The sentence in (16) also parses by the grammar (formally treating the second VP as an adjunct, as outlined above), but only relative to a transitive frame for *su* corresponding to the meaning 'bewitch'.

For a language with many multiverb construction types, it might be tried to feed total expressions like (5) into the verb frame of the first verb, and construe also the formal adjunct as 'foreseen' by the head verb, and thus separating the technical combination frame from what is intuitively a valence frame. This, however, is not a possibility that the present grammar ventures into.

To have an impression of how frequently a multiverb expression may be associated with a given verb, the following table indicates how often the types SVC (as 'sv'), EVC (as 'ev') and Verbid construction (as 'trVid' or 'intrVid') are among the environments in which a verb can occur (for instance, 14 verb lexemes can occur in both intransitive, transitive and SVC environment), according to the resource built on Dakubu (unpublished a):

Table 1 Distribution of verbs over valence frames and construction types in Ga

{tr}	144
{intr}	51
{intr,tr}	44
{tr,ev}	23
{tr,sv}	15
{ev}	15
{intr,tr,sv}	14
{tr,ditr}	9
{intr,tr,ev}	6
{intr,tr,ditr}	6
{tr,ditr,ev}	6
{intr,intrVid,tr}	6
{tr,ditr,sv}	5
{intr,tr,ev,sv}	4
{intr,tr,trVid,ditr,ev,sv}	4
{intr,tr,ditr,ev,sv}	4
{intrComp,tr}	3
{tr,ev,sv}	3
{intr,tr,ditr,sv}	3
{tr,trVid}	3
{ditr,ev}	3
{intr,tr,ditr,ev}	2
{intrVid,tr,sv}	2
{intrVid,tr}	2
{intrVid,tr,trVid}	2
{tr,ditr,ev,sv}	2
{intr,tr,trComp}	2

Calibrating these kinds of multiverb environments into a lexicon or grammar resource otherwise will be among the interesting next steps in dealing with digital resources for Volta Basin Kwa languages.

5. The grammar and its environment

As said above, a first version of the Ga grammar follows the formal architecture of Pollard and sag (1994), as used in many grammars adopting the Grammar matrix as a common feature structure repertory (Bender et a. (2010)). The later version, as illustrated here, has a simpler feature structure, which aims at more directly accommodating variation among languages. A guide to its feature structure is given in the pdf 'Building Global Grammar', which takes as point of departure a simple introductory grammar for English used as illustration in Copestake (2002), and stepwise builds up what is there called a 'global' feature structure, both with implementations and description. The description can be accessed at https://typecraft.org/tc2wiki/TypeGram, with a link from the Introduction, while the implementation is linked from http://regdili.hf.ntnu.no:8081/typegramusers/menu, with instructions at the TypeGram site. The specifications concerning Ga sit in a common repository of features covering also Germanic (Norwegian[14]), Bantu (Luganda) and Ethio-semitic (Kistaninya), as illustrated in Figure 5, here with a highlight on the Ga grammar ('GaGram'):

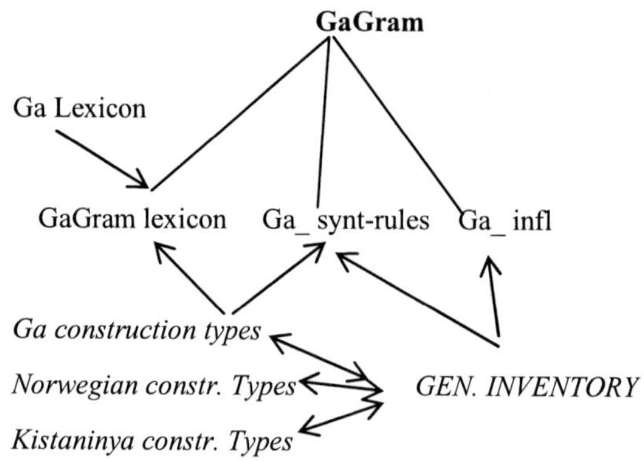

Figure 5 Architecture of resources

Among applications surrounding the grammar system is a procedure for grammar induction from Interlinear Glossed text (IGT), described in Hellan and Beermann (2011, 2014) and Bruland 2011, schematically indicated with an IGT snippet in (18):

(18)

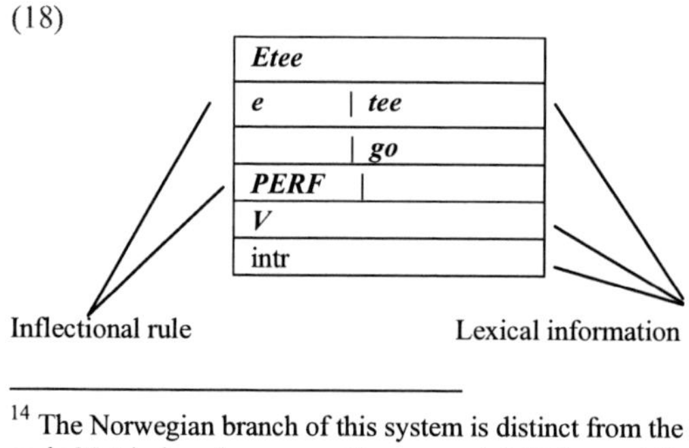

[14] The Norwegian branch of this system is distinct from the large scale Matrix-based grammar Norsource, (cf. Hellan and Bruland 2015), which has been maintained since 2001. Code files are downloadable from GitHub: https://github.com/Regdili-NTNU/NorSource/tree/master, and it has a web demo at http://regdili.hf.ntnu.no:8081/linguisticAce/parse. Also this grammar uses GF features, and its lexical types belong to the same system as what is presently described.

The inflectional rule here induced is

verb-Perf_irule := %prefix (* e) word & [TAM.T perf, DTR < v-lxm >],

and the lexical information induced is

tee-v := v-intr_lx & [ORTH <"tee">, ACTNT.PRED tee_rel].

In addition, one can also explore the GLOSS line specifications to obtain 'meta-string' versions of sentences of the language, in the case in point with

verb-Perf_irule := %prefix (* PERF) word & [TAM.T perf, Stem < v-lxm >].

as inflectional rule and

go-v := v-intr_lx & [ORTH <"go">, ACTNT.PRED go_rel].

as lexical information induced. Both courses are described at https://typecraft.org/tc2wiki/TypeGram. The latter course instantiates a procedure where the modules of syntactic and semantic parsing can be conducted separate from morphology. [15] Thus, relative to a sentence like (19),

(19)

Amɛ-wo	tsɔne	lɛ	mli	yɛlɛ
3P.AOR-put	vehicle	DEF	inside	yam
V	N	Art	N	N

'They put vehicle's inside yam' = 'They put yams in the lorry.'

such a 'meta' approach will address the construction in the shape (20a) rather than (20b):

(20) a. 3P*put*Aor *vehicle* DEF *inside yam*
b. *Amɛ-wo tsɔne lɛ mli yɛlɛ*

This method sustains a use of 145 sentences on the format of (20a) serving as an intermediate test suite for the full set of valence and construction types described in Hellan and Dakubu (2010).

6. Ga valence and verb construction dictionary

The Ga valence dictionary resources are represented as Dakubu (unpublished a) as a conversion from the enriched Toolbox version described in section 4, and in Dakubu (unpublished b) as a larger monograph. The material in Dakubu (unpublished a) is also online accessible as part of MultiVal, a comparative valence resource based on lexicons from LKB grammars for four languages.[16]

The point where this resource fits into the view of Figure 5 is, through its use of the CL labeling, marking its place within a compact cross-linguistic comparison of *language valence profiles*, which are enumerations of the valence and construction frames realized in a language. Preliminary comparisons of valence profiles for Ga and English suggest that they have less than 20% of their valency frames in common (see, e.g, Dakubu and Hellan (2016, 2017)).

[15] See Dakubu (2002) on the tone system, whose lexical and syntactic impact is not yet reflected in the grammar.

[16] Cf. Hellan et al (2014). Online site: http://regdili.hf.ntnu.no:8081/multilanguage_valence_demo/multivalence

An investigation of valence types in Ga can be related to the research into valence classes started with Levin 1993, followed up, i.a., in VerbNet and in the Leipzig Valency Classes (LVC) Project,[17] being attempts to associate commonalities in morpho-syntactic patterns with semantic factors, both language internally (like Levin and VerbNet) and cross-linguistically (LVC). Establishing valency classes for Ga has a tie to VerbNet in aiming at a fairly large coverage of the language's verbs,[18] and to LVC in establishing one more coordinate point in the attempt to attain a typologically broad basis for generalizations within this domain.

Given the large discrepancies in valence frames between Ga and English, a good strategy may be to first explore commonalities between Ga and other West African languages[19]. In the present setting, a natural step will for instance be to build a mapping between Ga and Akan lexical information, assuming that the valence labels used for Ga are adequate also for Akan.[20]

7. Conclusion

The view taken on the creation of a 'deep' computational grammar is that it allows one to

(i) through execution, create a formally tractable representation of structures of the language, where the execution binds one to consistency:

(ii) reflect on what are the essential structures of the grammar studied, and their relation to structures of other languages for which similar formally consistent investigations have been made;

(iii) effectively port one's findings to, or into the creation of, other resources.

Not least in the setting of African languages, an additional concern is to identify efficient ways of utilizing existing linguistic resources for the language in question, combined with a formal framework allowing for proper representation of the facts.

For languages with few previous digital facilities, a goal is to be able to develop a number of resources and applications in interaction but at a speed which allows one to digest and actively explore given and new connections. This is the goal of the resources here described, and we have highlighted the role of Prof. Dakubu's lexical resources, the way a grammar's organization of lexical information can lead to further resources, and we have discussed bearings that linguistic structures of Ga, and presumably Volta Basin Kwa in general, have on the formal structures of a grammar framework.

[17] Cf. for LVC, Malchukov and Comrie (eds) 2015 and http://valpal.info/; for VerbNet http://verbs.colorado.edu/~mpalmer/projects/verbnet.html.

[18] It is worth noting that while the VerbNet resource is essentially just a knowledge base, the present system is also used as an integral part of a syntactic parser.

[19] Perspectives are offered in Atoyebi (2015), Schaefer and Egbokhare. (2015), Creissels (2015), in the frame of LVC.

[20] Cf. Beermann and Hellan (2018) and (to appear).

8. Bibliographical References

Atoyebi, Joseph Dele Valency classes in Yorùbá. In: Malchukov, A., and B. Comrie (eds), pages 299-326.

Beermann, Dorothee, and Lars Hellan. 2018. West African Serial verb constructions: the case of Akan and Ga. In: Agwuele, Augustine, and Adams Bodomo (eds) *The Routledge Handbook of African Linguistics*. London and New York: Routledge. Pg. 207-221.

Beermann, D. and L. Hellan. To appear. Enhancing grammar and valence resources for Akan and Ga

Bender, Emily.M., Drellishak, S., Fokkens, A., Poulson, L. and Saleem, S. 2010. Grammar Customization. In *Research on Language & Computation*, Volume 8, Number 1, 23-72.

Bruland, T. (2011). Creating TypeGram data from TypeCraft. Presentation at *India 2011*, NTNU.

Copestake, Ann. 2002. *Implementing Typed Feature Structure Grammars*. CSLI Publications.

Creissels, Denis. 2015. Valency properties of Mandinka verbs. In: Malchukov, A., and B. Comrie (eds) Pages 221-260

Dakubu, M.E. Kropp, 2002. *Ga Phonology*. Institute of African Studies, Legon, Ghana.

Dakubu, M.E. Kropp, 2004a. The Ga preverb *kɛ* revisited. In Dakubu and Osam, eds., *Studies in the Languages of the Volta Basin* 2: 113-134. Legon: Linguistics Dept.

Dakubu, M.E. Kropp, 2004b. Ga clauses without syntactic subjects. *Journal of African Languages and Linguistics* 25.1: 1-40.

Dakubu, M.E. Kropp, 2008 Ga verb features. In Ameka and Dakubu eds., *Aspect and Modality in Kwa Languages.* Amsterdam & Philadelphia: John Benjamins Publishing Co. p. 91-134.

Dakubu, M. E. Kropp, 2009. *Ga-English Dictionary with English-Ga Index.* Accra: Black Mask Publishers

Dakubu, Mary Esther Kropp. Unpublished a. 'Ga_verb_dictionary_for_digital_processing'. Accessed for download at: https://typecraft.org/tc2wiki/Ga_Valence_Profile

Dakubu, Mary Esther Kropp. Unpublished b. Ga Verbs and their constructions. Monograph ms, Univ. of Ghana.

Dakubu, M.E.K., L. Hellan and D. Beermann. 2007. Verb Sequencing Constraints in Ga: Serial Verb Constructions and the Extended Verb Complex. In St. Müller (ed) *Proceedings of the 14th International Conference on Head-Driven Phrase Structure Grammar.* Stanford: CSLI Publications. (/http://csli-publications.stanford.edu/)

Dakubu, M.E. Kropp and Lars Hellan. 2016. Verb Classes and Valency classes in Ga. Paper read at Symposium on West African Languages (SyWAL) II, Vienna.

Dakubu, M.E. Kropp and Lars Hellan. 2017. A labeling system for valency: linguistic coverage and applications. In Hellan, L., Malchukov, A., and Cennamo, M (eds) *Contrastive studies in Valency.* Amsterdam & Philadelphia: John Benjamins Publ. Co.

Hellan, Lars. 2019a. Construction-Based Compositional Grammar. March 2019. *Journal of Logic Language and Information.* DOI: 10.1007/s10849-019-09284-5

Hellan, Lars and M.E. Kropp Dakubu. 2010. *Identifying verb constructions cross-linguistically*. In *Studies in the Languages of the Volta Basin* 6.3. Legon: Linguistics Department, University of Ghana.

Hellan, Lars, and Dorothee Beermann. 2014. Inducing grammars from IGT. In Z. Vetulani and J. Mariani (eds.) *Human Language Technologies as a Challenge for Computer Science and Linguistics.* Springer.

Hellan, L., D. Beermann, T. Bruland, M.E.K. Dakubu, and M. Marimon. 2014. *MultiVal*: Towards a multilingual valence lexicon. In Calzolari, Nicoletta et al. (eds.) Proceedings of the 9th International Conference on Language Resources and Evaluation (LREC 2014), pages 2785–2792, Reykjavík, Iceland. ELRA.

Hellan, Lars and Tore Bruland. 2015. A cluster of applications around a Deep Grammar. In: Vetulani et al. (eds) *Proceedings from The Language & Technology Conference* (LTC) 2015, Poznan.

Hirzel, Hannes. 2006. "Porting lexicon files from Toolbox into LKB-grammars: A case study for a grammar of Ga." https://typecraft.org/tc2wiki/File:Toolbox-LKB-Link-slides_-_version_4.pdf.

Levin, B. 1993. *English Verb Classes and Alternations.* Chicago IL: University of Chicago Press.

Malchukov, Andrej L. & Comrie, Bernard (eds.) (2015). *Valency classes in the world's languages.* Berlin: De Gruyter Mouton. 2015.

Pollard, Carl and Ivan Sag (1994) *Head-driven Phrase Structure Grammar.* Chicago Univ. Press.

Rask, R. 1828. *Vejledning til Akra-Sproget på Kysten Ginea* ('Introduction to the Accra language on the Guinea Coast').

Schaefer, R.B, and Francis O. Egbokhare. 2015. Emai valency classes and their alternations. In Malchukov, A. and B. Comrie (eds) 2015. Pp. 261-298.

9. Language Resource References

https://typecraft.org/tc2wiki/TypeGram

https://typecraft.org/tc2wiki/Ga_Valence_Profile

Proceedings of the First workshop on Resources for African Indigenous Languages (RAIL), pages 45–50
Language Resources and Evaluation Conference (LREC 2020), Marseille, 11–16 May 2020

Navigating Challenges of Multilingual Resource Development for Under-Resourced Languages: The Case of the African Wordnet Project

Marissa Griesel, Sonja Bosch
University of South Africa (UNISA)
Pretoria, South Africa
{griesm, boschse}@unisa.ac.za

Abstract

Creating a new wordnet is by no means a trivial task and when the target language is under-resourced as is the case for the languages currently included in the multilingual African Wordnet (AfWN), developers need to rely heavily on human expertise. During the different phases of development of the AfWN, we incorporated various methods of fast-tracking to ease the tedious and time-consuming work. Some methods have proven effective while others seem to have little positive impact on the work rate. As in the case of many other under-resourced languages, the expand model was implemented throughout, thus depending on English source data such as the English Princeton Wordnet (PWN) which is then translated into the target language with the assumption that the new language shares an underlying structure with the PWN. The paper discusses some problems encountered along the way and points out various possibilities of (semi) automated quality assurance measures and further refinement of the AfWN to ensure accelerated growth. In this paper we aim to highlight some of the lessons learnt from hands-on experience in order to facilitate similar projects, in particular for languages from other African countries.

Keywords: multilingual wordnet; under-resourced languages; African languages

1. Introduction

The African Wordnet (AfWN) project has as its aim the development of wordnets for indigenous languages, including Setswana, isiXhosa, isiZulu, Sesotho sa Leboa, Tshivenḓa, Sesotho, isiNdebele, Xitsonga and Siswati. The most recent development phase is funded by the South African Centre for Digital Language Resources (SADiLaR)[1] and runs from 2018 to the end of February 2020, with an extension to 2022 currently under consideration. A next version of the AfWN language resources is currently being prepared for distribution and will be made available under the same conditions and on the same platform as the first versions for the initial five languages (UNISA, 2017). Also see Bosch and Griesel (2017) for a detailed description.

While the focus in the past was on the official South African languages, the project also strives to establish a network of projects across Africa with teams representing other African languages adding their own wordnets. In this presentation we hope to share some of the unique challenges and obstacles encountered during the development of a technically complex resource with very limited to no additional natural language processing (NLP) tools. We discuss examples of linguistic idiosyncrasies and suggest ways to represent these examples in a formal database such as a wordnet. Furthermore, we also look at some common pitfalls when using English (UK or US) as source language for manual resource development, opening the floor to further discussion between language experts, developers and users of African language resources so as to ensure the usefulness thereof within the rapidly expanding African human language technology (HLT) and digital humanities (DH) spheres.

2. Background

2.1 The AfWN Project

Ordan and Wintner (2007) as well as Vossen *et al.* (2016) describe two common methods used to develop wordnets, based on the number and size of additional resources available, the experience of the team and the underlying grammatical structure of the language being modelled. The *merge approach* is popular for new wordnets with ample additional resources such as bilingual dictionaries, descriptive grammars and text corpora. Wordnets are constructed independently from any existing wordnets as a stand-alone resource, after which a separate process is followed to align the newly created wordnet with the Princeton WordNet (PWN) (Princeton University, 2020; and Fellbaum, 1998). PolNet, a Polish wordnet (Vetulani *et al.* 2010) that is based on a high-quality monolingual Polish lexicon, is a good example of a project following this approach. In the case of less-resourced languages, the PWN can be used as template in which to develop a new wordnet. This is referred to as the *expand model* according to which the source wordnet, usually the English PWN, is translated into the target language, with the assumption that the new language shares an underlying structure with the PWN. The Croatian Wordnet is an example of a wordnet based on the expand model due to a lack of semantically organized lexicons (cf. Raffaelli et al., 2008:350).

Typically, wordnets following this approach do not have access to many other digital resources and rely heavily on the linguistic knowledge of the development team. The AfWN project also followed the latter approach to build wordnets for the indigenous languages in a staggered but parallel manner. Initially, the project only included four languages – isiZulu, isiXhosa, Setswana and Sesotho sa Leboa – to allow the team to gain experience and to set up the infrastructure for further expansion. Once the project

[1] https://www.sadilar.org/

was established and more funding was secured, Tshivenḓa and later the remaining languages were added. The team also initially focussed on only providing usage examples to the basic synsets (including a lemma, part of speech and domain tags) and only during a third development stage

started adding definitions to the existing synsets[2]. Some of the languages had more resources available than others and the next section will give a brief overview of the different experiments performed to utilise as many available resources as possible.

2.2 Limited Available Resources for Some Languages

As reported in Griesel & Bosch (2014) initial manual development of the wordnets was a time consuming and tedious process. Not only were the team still learning the finer details of this type of language resource development, but linguists had to choose which synsets to translate without much help from electronic resources and only added roughly 1000 synsets per language per year. It was clear that more creative ways to speed up the development would have to be implemented if the project were to grow to a useful size within a practical time frame. It is also important to note again that almost all the linguists and language experts making up the AfWN team were working on this project on a part-time basis. Any degree of fast-tracking would therefore also be beneficial in easing their workload.

One experiment included using very basic bilingual wordlists found on the internet to identify synsets in the PWN that could be included in the AfWN semi-automatically. It involved matching an English term with the most likely PWN synset and then extracting the applicable English information such as a definition, usage example and classification tags from that synset into a spreadsheet with the African language translation of the lemma. Linguists then could easily translate these sheets before they were again included in the wordnet structure in the same position as the identified PWN synset. Griesel & Bosch (2014) give a complete overview of the resources that were used for Setswana, Sesotho sa Leboa, Tshivenḓa, isiXhosa and isiZulu to add just over 8000 new synsets to the AfWN.

Unfortunately, this method could not be followed for all languages as a basic resource such as freely available, digital, bilingual wordlists do not even exist for all the South African languages. Linguists have to rely solely on their own knowledge, underpinned by commercial (hardcopy) dictionaries and private databases. For these language teams, working in groups with constant communication between the linguists was essential as they performed the mostly manual development task.

3. The SILCAWL List

3.1 SILCAWL List as Alternative to Other Seed Lists

Another key challenge for the AfWN project was deciding on which concepts to include at which stage of development. It may seem logical to move alphabetically through the English source data and simply translate every synset but taking into consideration the capacity available in the project, this decision becomes less trivial. As mentioned previously, the project depends heavily on part-time team members and also on securing funding for limited periods of time. To translate all 250 000 synsets in the PWN would therefore take years and the AfWN would not be very useful for further NLP applications until the complete A – Z translation has been performed. As we later discuss in section 5, many lexical gaps exist between the PWN and the African languages and including only synsets also found in (American) English would result in a very flat meaning representation in the AfWN, with many concepts unique to the African context being omitted.

At the onset of the AfWN project, the team followed the example of many other wordnet projects such as the Catalan wordnet (Benítez *et al.* 1998) and the IndoWordnet project (Prabhu *et al.* 2012) and started with the translation of the so called "common base concepts" (CBC; created in the BalkaNet project[3]). This list is regarded as the building block for common semantic relations and is derived from comparing frequency lists for all of the Balkan languages included in that project to find the common set of 5 000 concepts to use as seed list (Weisscher, 2013). However, as discussed in Griesel *et al.* (2019) it soon became apparent that this Eurocentric list would not be ideal for further use in the AfWN project as it contained many concepts that were not lexicalised in the African languages.

Upon further research, the development team decided to employ the SIL Comparative African Wordlist (SILCAWL), which was compiled in 2006 by Keith Snider (SIL International and Canada Institute of Linguistics) and James Roberts (SIL Chad and Université de N'Djaména). This bilingual English-French wordlist includes 1 700 words compiled after extensive linguistic research in Africa. An interesting comparison between the usefulness of the CBC and the SILCAWL lists for expansion of the AfWN is drawn in Griesel *et al.* (2019) indicating that the SILCAWL list to be much better suited to the needs of the AfWN. The most significant enhancement is observed against the background of localisation where the content (of the entries) is lexicalised within an African environment, thereby guarding against datasets that may perpetuate culturally and cognitively biased language resources. This list was therefore used, not only to expand the five languages that formed part of the first two development stages, but also as starting point for the remaining four languages added in the most recent third stage. Xitsonga, Sesotho, Siswati and isiNdebele would therefore include as their first synsets entries from this more localised list.

3.2 Translation Procedure

In an effort to fast-track development, it was decided to first add (South African) English definitions and usage examples to the SILCAWL list and then to translate the data into the African languages. The first step would be done by an English lexicographer and expert translators

[2] See Bosch and Griesel (2017) as well as Griesel et al. (2019) for a detailed description of the development process followed thus far.

[3] See http://www.dblab.upatras.gr/balkanet/

rather than our core project team, where possible, allowing the different tasks to run simultaneously and thereby saving time.

The SILCAWL list only contains an English and a French lemma with very little information by which to disambiguate the implied meaning. In order to maintain the mapping to the PWN as far as possible, the first step was to determine which of the lemmas are included in the PWN and to extract all possible synsets for each lemma. Each candidate synset was then scrutinised manually by the development team and the best possible meaning representation selected from the possible senses. The PWN ID, definition and usage example (where available) were also added to the SILCAWL list. 41 SILCAWL lemmas were however not found in the PWN at all and the definitions or usage examples for many of the other lemmas needed revision in order to create a standardised, localised English dataset that could be translated to the African languages.

The project team, who are experienced wordnet developers after more than 13 years in the AfWN, next used the resulting translations to create synsets, complete with semantic relations in WordnetLoom (cf. Naskret et al., 2018), an open wordnet editor, with elaborated visualization for wordnet structures. The project team would also still work in teams of at least two language experts for each language so as to perform manual verification and quality assurance on the AfWN content throughout the development process.

An AfWN style guide was drawn up and sent to both the English lexicographer as well as the African language translators. This document included details on the translation and formatting of usage examples and definitions, including guidelines on the following aspects:

- No sentence initial capitalisation or punctuation at the end of a sentence is to be included;
- A specific tag should be used to reference definitions taken from the Open Educational Resource Term Bank (OERTB[4]);
- Examples of well formulated definitions and usage examples;
- A reminder not to include any usage examples from proprietary sources such as dictionaries;
- The lemma or head word of a synset also needs to be included in the usage example, but not in the definition;
- etc.

4. Evaluation of Translations

During discussions with linguists regarding the new synsets created from the expanded and translated SILCAWL list, many language-specific as well as general concerns were raised. The most notable two categories of concerns were those of a technical nature where the style guide was not adhered to or where mandatory fields were filled incorrectly, as well as issues that had to do with differences between the English source language and the nine African target languages. Some examples of each category as well as important decisions made are discussed below.

4.1 Technical Errors

Smrz (2004) as well as Miháltz *et al.* (2008) describe several ways to perform automatic and semi-automatic quality assurance on wordnets. These heuristics involve structural checks such as making sure only valid values are entered into specified fields (for instance for the POS, SUMO and MILO domains and semantic relations) which need to be referred back to a language expert for revision, as well as formatting checks (for instance eliminating sentence initial capitalisation or sentence ending punctuation) which could be solved automatically. The development team also began initial experiments to incorporate many of these checks/corrections in simple SQL queries or scripts which will result in a more cohesive and standardised resource. Figure 1 shows some of the basic errors found in the isiZulu wordnet, including capitalisation and punctuation mistakes, duplicate usage examples and English usage examples in the African language field.

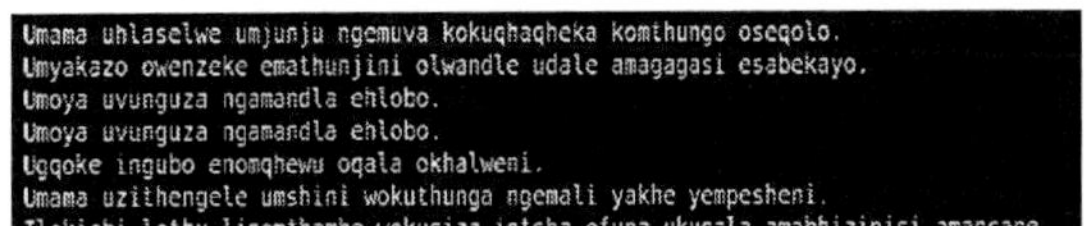

Figure 1. Automatic extraction of errors in the isiZulu wordnet.

It is envisioned that a language independent quality control pipeline could be established to incorporate these automatic and semi-automatic corrections. A simple user interface built on top of such a pipeline could present problematic synsets/fields to a language expert one at a time with options to accept an automatically generated correction or reject and manually correct possible errors. The second category of errors, namely language specific decisions, would be more complicated to identify automatically and would almost always require human intervention to solve.

4.2 Language Specific Decisions

4.2.1 Euphemisms

The African languages often make use of euphemisms to refer to taboo terms, especially terms related to the human body. One such example in Xitsonga is for the concept of "breaking wind/farting" where the biological translation would be *tamba* but the preferred euphemism is *humesa moya* – literally translated as "to kill an insect". In isiZulu, the biological term for "clitoris" is *umsunu*, however, *ubhontshisi*, the euphemism literally meaning "bean", is preferred. Discussions with the translators and the wordnet experts made it clear that, although the scientific term exists, it is very rarely used and considered vulgar and inappropriate language in most contexts. The team therefore decided to include both terms – the taboo and the euphemism – with a tag marking them as such in the wordnet.

[4] See http://oertb.tlterm.com/about/

4.2.2 Lexical Gaps or Lexicalisations Between English and the African Languages

A typical example of lexical gaps existing in the PWN, is the intricate system of kinship terms in the African languages that needs to be made provision for in the AfWN. The following table provides a few examples that demonstrate how the English kinship relations "uncle" and "aunt", as well as the "in-laws" need to be expanded for the target languages isiZulu and Sesotho sa Leboa in the AfWN (also cf. Griesel et al., 2019):

SILCAWL	ISIZULU	SESOTHO SA LEBOA
BLOOD RELATIONS		
0348 father's brother (uncle)	*ubabamkhulu* (big father) 'father's elder brother' *ubabomncane* (small father) - 'father's younger brother'	*ramogolo* 'father's elder brother' *rangwane* 'father's younger brother'
0351 father's sister (aunt)	*ubabekazi* (female father) 'father's sister'	*rakgadi* 'father's sister'
0349 mother's brother (uncle)	*umalume* (male mother) 'mother's brother'	*malome* 'mother's brother'
0350 mother's sister (aunt)	*umamekazi* (female mother) or *umame* 'mother's sister'	*mmamogolo* 'mother's elder sister' *mmane* 'mother's younger sister'
MARRIAGE RELATIONS		
0365 father-in-law	*ubabezala* 'father-in-law' used by Zulu-speaking woman *umukhwe* 'father-in-law' used by Zulu-speaking man	*ratswale* 'father-in-law'
0366 mother-in-law	*umkhwekazi* 'mother-in-law' used by Zulu-speaking man *umamezala* 'mother-in-law' used by Zulu-speaking woman	*mmatswale* / *mogwegadi* 'mother-in-law' (man speaking – dialectal) *mmatswale* 'mother-in-law' (woman speaking)
0367 brother-in-law	*umfowethu* 'husband's brother' *umkhwenyawethu* 'sister's husband' (man speaking) *umlamu* 'wife's brother' *umkhwenyana* 'sister's husband' (woman speaking)	*molamo, sebara* 'sister's husband' (man and woman speaking) *molamo, sebara* 'wife's brother' (man speaking)
0368 sister-in-law	*udadewethu* 'husband's sister' *umakoti, umlobokazi, umkami* 'brother's wife' (man speaking) *umlamu* 'wife's sister' *umakoti womfowethu, umakoti womnewethu* 'brother's wife' (woman speaking)	*mogadibo* 'husband's sister'/ 'brother's wife'

Table 1. Lexical gaps between the source language English and the target languages isiZulu and Sesotho sa Leboa.

With regard to lexicalisation in the African languages, an example in isiZulu is the verb *finya* "blowing the nose". This example of lexicalisation prevents the noun *ikhala* "nose" from featuring in the usage example:

1. nose ENG20-05278188-n ikhala
   "blow your nose after you sneeze"
   finya emuva kokuthimula

Translating from English to isiZulu without knowledge of the wordnet structure and the stipulated guideline that the usage example needs to include the lemma, results in a semantically acceptable sentence but would confuse a user of the wordnet. In other words, a more suitable usage example should be suggested by the linguist, e.g.

2. "the boxer injured his nose"
   umlobi wesibhakela walimala ekhaleni lakhe

Numerous examples of concepts that are not lexicalised in the African languages were also encountered. Linguists who were unfamiliar with wordnet development and deemed it necessary to adhere stringently to the CBC list then included descriptions of these terms comprising up to 7 words as the lemma, rather than choosing a more suitable PWN sense or omitting the synset completely in the African language. This took valuable time and lead to frustration on the side of the linguists as they were constantly busy coining new descriptions rather than adding more frequently used concepts to the wordnet. The English concept of a "complication" (ENG20-13271751-n; any disease or disorder that occurs during the course of (or because of) another disease) was for instance translated as *izinkinga zokugula ezidalwa ukuba khona kokunye ukugula*, literally meaning "disease problems caused by the presence of another disease".

5. Suggestions for Improvement

Given the types of stumbling blocks and language specific idiosyncrasies observed throughout the development process, including quality assurance, the project team suggests the following improvements in the protocol. Some of these aspects were immediately implemented while some will require future work.

One of the first measures to improve the translated data to better fit the wordnet application, is to make sure that the English lexicographer as well as the African language translators are well informed about the ultimate use of their work. The style guide was expanded to include updated instructions and examples of suitable definitions and usage examples. A section was also added on quality assurance and the types of errors to be especially mindful of. Since the linguists all work in the AfWN project on a part-time basis, the team is constantly growing to include more linguists or replace those who no longer have time available. Continuous training of new linguists at the hand of the extended style guide is therefore more effective as well.

Adding morphological analysis or lemmatisation in the pipeline for purposes of quality assurance, for instance in order to verify that the lemma or head word of a synset is included in the usage example, requires further experimentation but will greatly reduce the amount of confusing usage examples. In direct searches, the lemma or head word can easily be obscured by inflection and morphophonological alternations, particularly in conjunctively written languages. For instance, in the following examples:

3. isiZulu
   thigh ENG20-05243922-n *ithanga*
   "she has a huge bruise on her thigh"
   unomhuzuko omkhulu ethangeni lakhe

The noun *ithanga* "thigh" is used in the locative form in the usage example, viz. *ethangeni*.

4. isiXhosa
   perspire, sweat ENG20-00065374-v *bila*
   "exercise makes one sweat"
   ezemithambo ziyambilisa umntu

The verb *ziyambilisa* "it causes one to sweat" is used with the causative suffix or verb extension *-is-*.

As a future goal, the team is also planning to include (semi) automatic quality assurance measures directly into the development interface. Morphological analysis as mentioned above, spelling correction, checking for empty fields and allowed categories can all be done in-line. Suggestions/prompts before saving can be added to the interface as a final step before a linguist signs off on a specific synset. We further envision enhancing the interface with improved internal communication so that a linguist can send comments on a synset directly to a team member for verification. Having a full record of the (linguistic) decisions made will also help improve the protocol for development and will offer valuable insights to new wordnet projects so that there is no need to "reinvent the wheel".

6. Conclusion

All data developed in the AfWN project will be made available under a Creative Commons license[5] via the SADiLaR language resource repository with the hope that it can increase NLP development particularly for the African languages. It is important for users of the data to be aware of certain linguistic and technical decisions made during development so that they can also make provision for certain aspects in their systems.

Since so many wordnets for under-resourced, linguistically complex languages follow the expand method for wordnet development and rely heavily on the English source data as in the PWN, it is further important to document the lexical gaps and applicable differences between languages. We hope that by doing so in the project documentation and in publications, that we can facilitate the accelerated growth of the AfWN to include languages from other African countries.

7. Acknowledgements

The African Wordnet project (AfWN) was made possible with support from the South African Centre for Digital Language Resources (SADiLaR), a research infrastructure established by the Department of Science and Technology of the South African government as part of the South African Research Infrastructure Roadmap (SARIR).

The authors would also like to acknowledge and thank the linguists and technical project members involved in the AfWN project. A list of significant contributors is available on the project webpage (https://africanwordnet.wordpress.com/team/).

8. Bibliographical References

Benítez, L., Cervell, S., Escudero, G., López, M., Rigau, G. and Taulé, M. (1998). Methods and tools for building the Catalan Wordnet. In ELRA (ed.). *Proceedings of the First International Conference on Language Resources and Evaluation (LREC'98)*, Granada, Spain, May 28–30. Available at http://www.cs.upc.edu/~escudero/wsd/98-lrec.pdf.

Bosch, S. and Griesel, M. (2017). Strategies for building wordnets for under-resourced languages: the case of African languages. *Literator* 38(1), a1351. Available at https://doi.org/10.4102/lit.v38i1.1351

Fellbaum, C. (ed). (1998). *Wordnet: An electronic lexical database*. The MIT Press, Cambridge, Mass.

Griesel, M. and Bosch, S. (2014). Taking stock of the African Wordnet project: 5 years of development. In Fellbaum, C. *et al.* (eds.) *Proceedings of the Seventh Global WordNet Conference 2014* (GWC2014), pp. 148-153. Tartu, Estonia. Available at http://gwc2014.ut.ee/proceedings_of_GWC_2014.pdf

Miháltz, M., Hatvani, C., Kuti, J., Szarvas, G., Csirik, J., Prószéky, G. and Váradi, T. (2008). Methods and results of the hungarian wordnet project. In: Tanács, A., *et al.* (eds). *Proceedings of the 4th Global WordNet Conference (GWC2008)*, pp. 311-320. Szeged,

[5] See https://creativecommons.org/licenses/

Hungary. Available at http://www.inf.u-szeged.hu/projectdirs/gwc2008/

Naskręt, T., Dziob, A., Maciej, P., Maciej, S., Chakaveh and Branco, A. (2018). WordnetLoom - a Multilingual Wordnet Editing System Focused on Graph-based Presentation. In: Fellbaum, C, *et al.* (eds). *Proceedings of Ninth Global WordNet Conference 2018 (GWC2018)*. Nanyang Technological University (NTU), Singapore. Available at http://compling.hss.ntu.edu.sg/events/2018-gwc/pdfs/gwc-2018-proceedings.pdf

Ordan, N. and Wintner, S. (2007). Hebrew WordNet: A test case of aligning lexical databases across languages. *International Journal of Translation, special issue on Lexical Resources for Machine Translation* 19(1), 39–58.

Prabhu, V., Desai, S., Redkar, H., Prabhugaonkar, N., Nagvenkar, A. and Karmali, R. (2012). An efficient database design for IndoWordNet development using hybrid approach. *Proceedings of the 3rd Workshop on South and Southeast Asian Natural Language Processing* (SANLP) at COLING 2012, Mumbai, December, pp. 229–236.

Raffaelli, I., Tadić, M., Bekavac, B. and Agić, Z. (2008). Building Croatian WordNet. In: Tanács, Attila, *et al.* (eds). *Proceedings of the 4th Global WordNet Conference (GWC2008),* pp. 311-320. Szeged, Hungary. Available at http://www.inf.u-szeged.hu/projectdirs/gwc2008/

Smrz, P. (2004). Quality Control and Checking for Wordnets Development: A Case Study of BalkaNet. In *Romanian Journal of Information Science and Technology Special Issue*, volume 7, No. 1-2.

Snider, K. and Roberts, J. (2006). *SIL Comparative African Wordlist (SILCAWL).* Available at https://www.eva.mpg.de/lingua/tools-at-lingboard/pdf/Snider_silewp2006-005.pdf)

Vetulani, Z., Kubis, M. and Obrębski, T. (2010). PolNet – Polish WordNet: Data and tools. In N. Calzolari, K. Choukri, B. Maegaard, J. Mariani, J. Odijk, S. Piperidis, et al. (eds.), *Proceedings of the Seventh International Conference on Language Resources and Evaluation (LREC'10),* Valletta, Malta, May 17–23, pp. 3739–3797.

Vossen, P., Bond, F. and McCrae, J. (2016). Toward a truly multilingual GlobalWordnet Grid. In Mititelu, V. *et al.* (eds.). *Proceedings of the Eighth Global WordNet Conference 2016* (GWC2016). Bucharest, Romania. Available at http://www.racai.ro/p/gwc2016/

Weisscher, A. (2013). Global Wordnet Association base concepts. Available at http://globalwordnet.org/gwa-base-concepts/

9. Language Resource References

Princeton University. (2020). WordNet – A lexical database for English. Available at https://wordnet.princeton.edu/

University of South Africa (UNISA). 2017. Wordnets for isiXhosa (ISLRN 484-200-848-869-7), isiZulu (ISLRN 884-495-382-918-6), Setswana (ISLRN 609-257-955-359-4), Sesotho sa Leboa (ISLRN 639-836-685-202-8) and Tshivenḓa (ISLRN 193-390-599-634-9). African Wordnet Project, distributed via SADiLaR, 1.0. Available at https://repo.sadilar.org/handle/20.500.12185/7/browse?type=project&value=African+Wordnet+Project

Proceedings of the First workshop on Resources for African Indigenous Languages (RAIL), pages 51–56
Language Resources and Evaluation Conference (LREC 2020), Marseille, 11–16 May 2020

Building Collaboration-based Resources In Endowed African Languages: Case Of NTeALan Dictionaries Platform

Elvis MBONING[1 2], Daniel BALEBA[1], Jean Marc BASSAHAK[1],Ornella WANDJI[1]
NTeALan[1], ERTIM (INALCO)[2]
Tradex Makepe - Douala (Cameroon), 2 rue de Lille - Paris (France)
elvis.mboning@inalco.fr[2]
{levismboning, daniel.baleba, bassahak, ornella.wandji}@ntealan.org[1]

Abstract

In a context where open-source NLP resources and tools in African languages are scarce and dispersed, it is difficult for researchers to truly fit African languages into current algorithms of artificial intelligence. Created in 2017, with the aim of building communities of voluntary contributors around African native and/or national languages, cultures, NLP technologies and artificial intelligence, the NTeALan association has set up a series of web collaborative platforms intended to allow the aforementioned communities to create and administer their own lexicographic resources. In this article, we present on the one hand the first versions of the three platforms: the REST API for saving lexicographical resources, the dictionary management platform and the collaborative dictionary platform; on the other hand, we describe the data format chosen and used to encapsulate our resources. After experimenting with a few dictionaries and some users feedback, we are convinced that only collaboration-based approach and platforms can effectively respond to the production of good resources in African native and/or national languages.

Keywords: African languages, NLP, resources, xmlisation, collaboration, dictionaries, lexicography, open-source

1. Introduction

Language plays an important role in defining the identity and humanity of individuals. As Tunde Opeibi (Tunde, 2012) said "In Africa, evidence shows that language has become a very strong factor for ethno national identity, with the ethnic loyalty overriding the national interest". To date, the African continent has more than 2000 languages, more than two thirds of which are poorly endowed. Among the reasons justifying this observation, we can list:

- The lack of a strong linguistic policy in favor of these languages
- The absence of the majority of these languages in the digital space (social networks, online or mobile platform, etc.) and in the educational system (mainly described by (Tadadjeu, 2004) and (Don, 2010))
- The lack of open-source African linguistic resources (textual and oral), Natural Language Processing (NLP) and/or Natural Language Understanding (NLU) tools available for most of these languages
- The lack of experts in NLP, NLU and Artificial Intelligence (AI) trained in the continent and who are specialists in these languages
- The lack of open-source African linguistic resources (textual and oral) and NLP and/or NLU tools available for most of these languages

For several years now, artificial intelligence technologies, including those of NLP, have greatly contributed to the economic and scientific emergence of poorly endowed languages in northern countries, thanks to the availability of lexicography and terminography resources in sufficient quantity. African languages benefit very little from these intelligent tools because of the scarcity of structured data and collaborative platforms available for building linguistic and cultural knowledge bases. In order to meet this need and complement the initiatives already present on the continent ((De Pauw et al., 2009), (Mboning, 2016), (Vydrin, Valentin and Rovenchak, Andrij and Maslinsky, Kirill, 2016), (Abate et al., 2018), (Mboning, Elvis and NTeALan contributors, 2017), (Mangeot and Enguehard, 2011), (De Schryver, 2010), Afrilex association (Ruthven, 2005)), and also those from African, European and American research centers, NTeALan (New Technologies for African Languages), specialized in the development of NLP and NLU tools for teaching African languages and cultures, has set up a collaborative and open-source platform for building lexical resources for African national languages. Our main goal is to deal with languages spoken in French-speaking African countries.

This paper focuses on the development of African linguistics and cultural resources, which is an important starting point for the technological step forward of each African language. We describe our collaborative language resources platform focusing on lexicographic data. This platform is divided into three components: the open-source dictionary backup API (back-end), the dictionary management platform and the collaborative dictionary platform (fronts-end).

2. Context of the work

2.1. NTeALan project

Created in 2017[1] and managed by academics and the African Learned Society, NTeALan is an Association that

[1]Namely by Elvis Mboning (NLP Research Engineer at INALCO) and Jean Marc Bassahak (Contractor, Web designer and developer), who were later on joined by Jules Assoumou, Head of

works for the implementation of intelligent technological tools, for the development, promotion and teaching of African native and/or national languages. Our goals are to digitize, safeguard and promote these poorly endowed languages through digital tools and Artificial Intelligence. By doing so, we would like to encourage and help young Africans, who are willing to learn and/or teach their mother tongues, and therefore build a new generation of Africans aware of the importance and challenges of appropriating the languages and cultures of the continent. Another purpose of NTeALan's work is to provide local researchers and companies with data which could help them improve the quality of their services and work, hence building open-source African languages resources is one of our core projects.

2.2. NTeALan's approach: collaboration-based model

Our approach is exclusively based on the collaboration model (Holtzblatt and Beyer, 2017). We would like to allow African people to contribute to the development of their own mother tongues, under the supervision of specialists and academics of African languages. Our model involves setting up several communities: a community of speakers of these languages, a community of native specialists (guarantors of traditional, cultural and linguistic knowledge), a community of academics specialized in African linguistic technologies and a community of social, institutional and public partners. Grouped by languages, these communities work together with the same goal: building linguistic and cultural resources useful for research, technological and educational needs.

This approach applies to all NTeALan's internal projects, especially to the language resources platforms, as well as their representation.

3. NTeALan's language resource platforms

Our language resource platforms are divided into three parts: one independent architecture and two dependent architectures. The independent architecture serves not only the two others but also all NTeALan's projects as illustrated in figure 1.

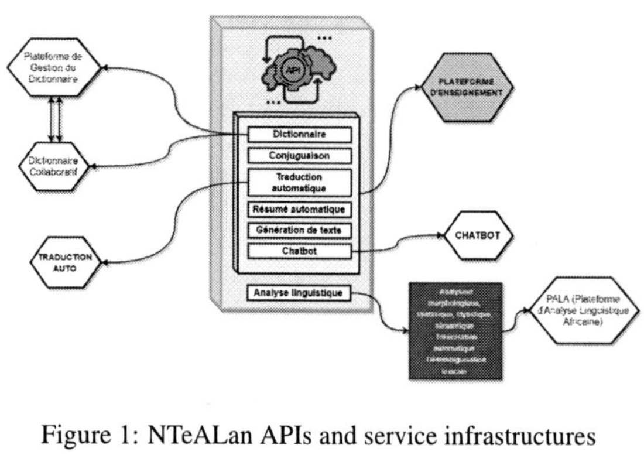

Figure 1: NTeALan APIs and service infrastructures

Department of Linguistics and African Literature at the University of Douala.

The three architectures are the fruit of two upstream processes depending on the input type (PDF files or images). The first process involves digitization and the second serialization:

- **digitization**: dictionaries in paper or digital format like PDF, TIFF, PNG by OCR (Optical Character Recognition) are digitized with Deep learning (Breuel, 2008); we annotate them to improve the OCR (see figure 2); each article constituents (featured word, translation, contextualization, conjugation, dialect variant, etc.) are automatically detected, extracted and xml-ized in XND (XML NTeALan Dictionary) format afterwards.
- **serialization**: dictionaries in an external format (toolbox, XML, TEI, LMF) are automatically serialized in XND format, using our internal NLP tools[2].

In both cases, we start with a paper or digital dictionary and end up with a XML dictionary in XND format. The latter is the unique data entry format for our three architectures. It should be noted that the two processes described above are controlled by NTeALan linguists only. In future work they will be opened to non-member contributors.

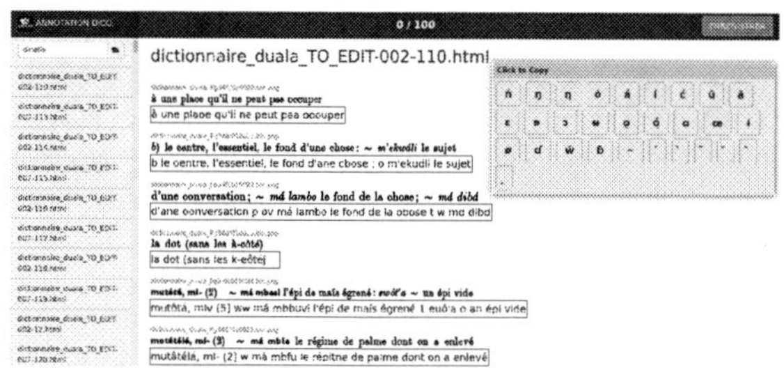

Figure 2: NTeALan dictionaries annotation platform based on Ocropy tool and used to train Deep learning model for OCR. This platform is under license on Creative Commons BY-NC-SA 3.0 license: (`http://dico-edit.ntealan.net`)

Figure 2 shows an example of annotation (from the bilingual Duala-French dictionary) performed by NTeALan's members.

3.1. Independent architecture

The independent platform is a web-based REST API platform. It can also be called lexicographical resources management database. Built to be simple and accessible, this web application stores and distributes all the lexicographic resources resulting from the collaborative work done by NTeALan's communities members and external contributors.

The independent architecture uses our internal NLP tools to manage the XND file format in order to give users easy

[2]These include tokenizers, lemmatizers, text parsers and lexical disambiguation tools used for processing noisy lexicographic corpora.

access to their contributions (see section 4.). The operations listed in table 3.1. are authorized in open access for each type of user.

Operations	NTeALan's users	Native speakers community	Scientific experts
manage dictionary	yes	no	yes
manage article	yes	yes	yes
validations	no	yes	yes
cultural media	yes	yes	no
comments	yes	yes	yes

Table 1: Users' privileges for each operation in NTeALan's REST API

This architecture is hosted at `https://apis.ntealan.net/ntealan/dictionaries` and is accessible under the Creative Commons BY-NC-SA 3.0 license. The access rights, for each type of user, is described in table 3.1..

3.2. Dependent architectures

Dependent architectures are web platforms which use the data stored in common REST API database (Independent platform), the latter are enriched by contributors. They can also perform the operations described in table 3.1. through their web interface.

3.2.1. Dictionaries management platform

As a web platform, the dictionaries management platform is a graphical management version of the REST API platform. It allows NTeALan members (users) to manage dictionaries, articles, users, users comments, access requests and cultural resources.

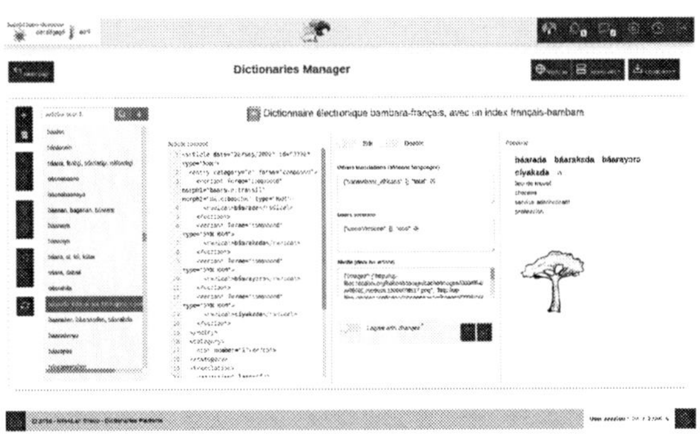

Figure 3: Dictionaries management platform for managing multi-modal and multilingual lexicographical resources in African languages. This platform is under NTeALan's license: (`https://ntealan.net/dictionaries-platform`)

Unlike the two above-mentioned platforms, this is not an open-source platform. It can be used strictly by NTeALan's communities, in a direct collaboration between the linguistics team members and other association members.

3.2.2. Collaborative dictionary platform

The collaborative dictionary[3] is also a web platform (see figure 4) which enriches the lexicographic resources from the REST API. It gives NTeALan's communities members (see section 2.2.), more precisely native speakers and African languages experts, the opportunity to build, in a collaborative approach, resources like lexicons[4], illustration of cultural phenomenon, sounds and videos (recording process) based on semantic information provided by article written in their native languages. These shared resources are stored and freely available for all contributors through our REST API.

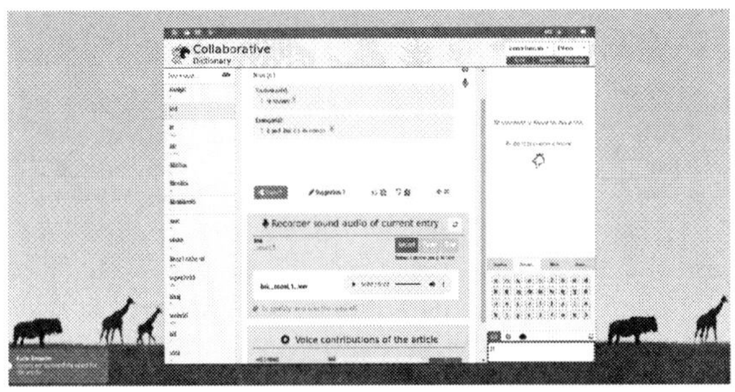

Figure 4: Collaborative dictionaries for sharing multi-modal and multilingual lexicographical resources in African languages. This platform is under Creative Commons BY-NC-SA 3.0 license: (`https://ntealan.net`)

4. NTeALan language resources and representation

Most of our dictionaries resources are old bilingual dictionaries (from linguists' work) found on the web as open-source or under Creative Commons BY-NC-SA 3.0 license. The references to the original sources and to the NTeALan's versions are provided on all our platforms from where they can also be consulted.

4.1. African language resource dictionaries

We currently host and share 7 bilingual dictionaries[5] on our REST API. Although the number of entries to date is

[3]This project was born following the research work of Elvis Mboning at the University of Douala and University of Lille 3 (Master thesis): (Mboning, 2016) and (Mboning, 2017). We can cite other related work to this field like (Assoumou, 2010), (Mangeot and Enguehard, 2011), (Vydrin et al., 2016), (Maslinsky, 2014), (Nouvel et al., 2016), etc.

[4]To this aim, we built another platform to manage lexicographic resource: [https://ntealan.net/dictionaries-platform].

[5]Although the first versions are bilingual, these dictionaries are meant to be multilingual, with priority being given to translation in all the foreign languages spoken in Africa.

still relatively limited (from 3 to 11,500 entries), a growing community is participating daily in their filling. Table 4.1. shows the current statistics on the resources managed by our API.

Language resources	Entries	Entries contrib.	Media contrib.
Bambara-French	11487	1	1
Yemba-French	3031	2	90
Bassa-French	427	5	5
Duala-French	191	5	0
Ghomala-French	16	1	0
Ngiemboon-French	3	2	1
Fulfulde-French	0	0	0

Table 2: State of the art of NTeALan language resources currently saved in the REST API

Even if the current resources are insufficient and cover only 7 sub-saharan languages, we are nevertheless satisfied with the craze that is beginning to appear within the communities of users behind our platforms. However we would like to determine whether our different infrastructures fit with the resources produced, the load of connected users and the users needs. Once we have completed the tests on the platform, the next steps will be generalizing the model to the other African languages included in our dictionaries.

4.2. Description of NTeALan's XML format

Each lexical resource management platform has its own model for structuring and presenting data (sample of (Mangeot, 2006) and (Benoit and Turcan, 2006)). The XML format (mainly TEI and LMF XML standards) is today a reference choice for structuring linguistic, lexicographic and terminographic data. However, it turns out that these standards are not often adapted to represent and describe African languages. Indeed, several linguistic phenomena such as the concept of nominal class, the management, translation and localisation of dialect variants, and the notion of clicks are not explicitly treated, despite all the needs expressed with regard to the matter[6].

After analyzing the structure of a Bantu language from Cameroon (Yemba, spoken in West region), we decided to define a proprietary XML structuring model, whose structure was inspired by the 4 major families of African languages, namely the Afro-Asian family, the Niger-Kordofan family, Nilo-Saharan family and the Koisan family. Three principles guided our choice: representation, simplification and extensibility:

- **representation**: this principle aims at describing language data at the smallest morpho-syntactic level i.e. word components (prefix+radical+suffix) and phrase components like class accord (1/2, 2/4, 5/7).

[6]Note that it is nonetheless possible in these standards to add new formalism (tags and attributes) in addition to existing classes.

- **simplification**: we try to choose XML tag names and international languages that are easily comprehensible for the research communities. Also, we decided to use a linear XML representation, with less parents and more children in the same parent node.

- **extensibility**: we would like to give external contributors the possibility to extend our main XML structure by adding new nodes (children or parent nodes), depending on the element to represent.

We design our *core-node* lexicographic data with a root node called <ntealan_dictionary>, which is divided into two subnodes: <ntealan_paratexte> and <ntealan_articles>. <ntealan_paratexte> describes the metadata about the version(s) of the document (context of the dictionaries production, source description of the original authors and target description of the XML VERSION). <ntealan_articles> describes all the dictionary articles (<article>).

Each article has its own subnodes: <entry> (dialect variant currently processed), <category> (grammatical categor(y/ies) associated to the dialect variant(s)), <translations> (translations associated to the dialect, <examples> (contextualisation of the dialect variants). Figure 5 illustrates this data representation.

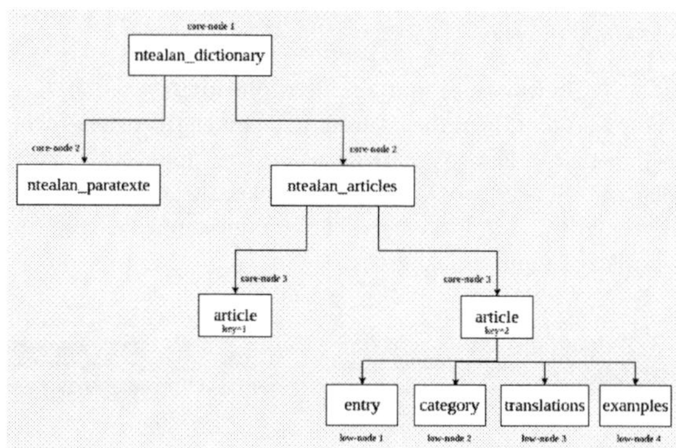

Figure 5: NTeALan dictionaries XML representation

The extension of the article structure by contributors is only possible in *low-node*, as shown in figures 5, 6 and 7, which means that the article model can be updated at each node level (referred to by an id).

Our XND format is not intended to be standardized to serve as a reference. On the contrary, it is used as intermediate format, required by our internal NLP tools and by well-known standardized formats. Indeed once the external formats are serialized in XND, we have the possibility to convert the data into other formats such as those of the TEI and LMF dictionaries. These features will be available at the API level soon.

```xml
<article type="Nom">
 <entry forme="simple">
   <variant type="YN" forme="simple">
     <prefix>m</prefix>
     <radical>bā</radical>
  </variant>
   <variant type="YS" forme="simple">
     <radical>mba-nnɛ́</radical>
  </variant>
</entry>
 <category>
   <cat number="1">n</cat>
</category>
 <classe_d_accords>
   <cl_sing number="1">9</cl_sing>
   <cl_plur number="1">10</cl_plur>
</classe_d_accords>
 <translations>
   <equivalent lang="fr" number="1">foureau</equivalent>
</translations>
</article>
```

Figure 6: Sample Xmlisation of nouns article *mbā* extracted from the Yemba-French dictionary

```xml
<article type="Verbe">
  <entry forme="simple">
    <variant type="YN" forme="simple">
      <prefix>le</prefix>
      <radical>baka</radical>
   </variant>
    <variant type="YS" forme="simple">
      <prefix>li</prefix>
      <radical>cu'o</radical>
   </variant>
 </entry>
  <category>
    <cat number="1">v</cat>
 </category>
  <conjugation>
    <conj_variant type="YN">
      <forme_conj type="2-F_infinitive">ḿbáká</forme_conj>
      <forme_conj type="imperative">báká</forme_conj>
   </conj_variant>
    <conj_variant type="YS">
      <forme_conj type="2-F_infinitive">ncú'ó</forme_conj>
      <forme_conj type="imperative">cú'o</forme_conj>
   </conj_variant>
 </conjugation>
  <translations>
    <equivalent lang="fr" number="1" emprunt_En="pack">
        entasser, accumuler
    </equivalent>
 </translations>
</article>
```

Figure 7: Sample Xmlisation of verbs article *lebaka* extracted from Yemba-French dictionary.

5. Problems encountered and future challenges

The implementation of these first platforms enabled us to take note of the main challenges. In upcoming years, we will focus on these issues, enriching our platforms and trying to improve them for future deadlines.

5.1. Problems encountered

We are currently facing two main problems with the NTeALan platforms:

- the first is the low number of contributors and the insufficient IT resources. The staff do not have all the specialists needed (in NLP, NLU and African languages) for the targeted goals and great ambitions. The current work is mainly carried out by 4 active members of the association. Regarding IT resources, we do not have enough robust IT infrastructures (servers, field tools, etc.) as required by such a research work on African languages.

- the second is the lack of funding to carry out our research activities with respect to the development of NLP and NLU tools. Our funding mainly comes from the contributions of the association members, which is not enough in the light of our current ambitions.

5.2. Further challenges

Our ambitions are great and will require more staff (language specialists) and financial resources. We would like to:

- Above all, encourage the greatest number of specialists in African languages and cultures from various African countries and in the whole world, to join our association because together we can easily take up challenges.

- Find funding from private and public institutions, businessmen, companies, who can support our research work and the continuous development of our applications for the teaching of poorly endowed African languages.

- Enrich and improve all existing platforms and open them up more to the scientific community and to speakers of the languages included. We will first of all focus on : the autonomous platform for language and culture teaching, the conversational Agent Assistant for Language Teaching and the Virtual cultural museum for safeguarding the African socio-cultural inheritance.

- Strengthen our partnerships with social and cultural African institutions, universities, research laboratories and companies specialized in our research areas. The aim is to create communities of experts in linguistics, technological and cultural issues throughout the continent.

De Schryver (De Schryver, 2010, p.587) already wondered about the specifics of electronic lexicography in the future in these terms: "The future of lexicography is digital, so much is certain. Yet what that digital future will look like, is far less certain.". This work clearly shows that the collaboration-based model, coupled with robust NLP platforms, could give meaning to the future nature of electronic lexicography in Africa.

6. Conclusion

In this article, we described NTeALan platforms and its XND data representation, and we showed how essential an association is nowadays, for the construction of good linguistic and lexicographic resources and tools for endowed African languages. We lead, internally with our academic partners (the language and African literature department of the University of Douala and the ERTIM team of INALCO (France)), numerous research activities in Artificial Intelligence, NLP, and NLU, in order to contribute to the industrialization of African languages. It is obvious that a lot remains to be done, however the first results of our study have proven to be very useful for our applications (the conversational agent NTeABot, the learning platform, the translation platform, etc.) and can be used by other researchers: this includes data (in different common formats like XML, TEI, LMF, XND) and tools. We are convinced, as Tunde Opeibi (Tunde, 2012, p.289) already said, that "the linguistic diversity in Africa can still become the catalyst that will promote cultural, socio-economic, political, and technological development, as well as sustainable growth and good governance in Africa."

7. Acknowledgements

These platforms was developed by Elvis Mboning (REST API and Dictionaries Management platform), Daniel Baleba (Collaborative dictionaries) and Jean-Marc Bassahak (Web Design and interfaces). NTeALan's projects are actually supported by the Ministry of Post and Telecommunication of Cameroon, the Department of linguistics and African literature of the University of Douala (Cameroon), the INALCO's ERTIM research team and Fractals system (France). We can also cite: Professor Jules Assoumou, Thanks to Christian Bonog Bilap, Marcel Tomi Banou, Ntomb David, Ntomb Nicolas, Théophile Kengne, Yves Bertrand Dissake, Juanita Fopa, Damien Nouvel and to the other contributors.

8. Bibliographical References

Abate, S. T., Melese, M., Tachbelie, M. Y., Meshesha, M., Atinafu, S., Mulugeta, W., Assabie, Y., Abera, H., Ephrem, B., Abebe, T., Tsegaye, W., Lemma, A., Andargie, T., and Shifaw, S. (2018). Parallel Corpora for bi-lingual English-Ethiopian Languages Statistical Machine Translation. In *Proceedings of the 27th International Conference on Computational Linguistics*, pages 3102–3111, Santa Fe, New Mexico, USA, August. Association for Computational Linguistics.

Assoumou, J. (2010). *Enseignement oral des langues et cultures africaines à l'école primaire*. Éditions Clé, Yaoundé, Cameroun, 1st edition.

Benoit, J.-L. and Turcan, I. (2006). La TEI au service de la transmission documentaire ou de la valorisation des richesses patrimoniales : le cas difficile des dictionnaires anciens.

Breuel, T. M. (2008). The OCRopus open source OCR system. *Proc.SPIE*, 6815.

De Schryver, G.-M. (2010). State-of-the-Art Software to Support Intelligent Lexicography. *ResearchGate*, page 16.

Don, O. (2010). African languages in digital space. *HSRC Press*, page 168.

Holtzblatt, K. and Beyer, H. (2017). 7 - Building Experience Models. pages 147–206, January.

Mangeot, M. and Enguehard, C. (2011). Informatisation de dictionnaires langues africaines-français. In *journées LTT 2011*, page 11.

Mangeot, M. (2006). Dictionary building with the jibiki platform. In Cristina Onesti Elisa Corino, Carla Marello, editor, *Proceedings of the 12th EURALEX International Congress*, pages 185–188, Torino, Italy, sep. Edizioni dell'Orso.

Maslinsky, K. (2014). *Daba: a model and tools for Manding corpora*.

Mboning, E. (2016). De l'analyse du dictionnaire yémba-français à la conception de sa DTD et de sa réédition sur support numérique. Mémoire Master 1, Université de Lille 3.

Mboning, E. (2017). Vers une métalexicographie outillée : conception d'un outil pour le métalexicographe et application aux dictionnaires Larousse de 1856 à 1966. Mémoire Master 2, Université de Lille 3.

Nouvel, D., Donandt, K., Auffret, D., Maslinsky, K., Chiarcos, C., and Vydrin, V. (2016). Resources and Experiments for a Bambara POS Tagger. *Intra Speech*, page 14.

Ruthven, R. (2005). The African Association for Lexicography: After Ten Years. *Lexikos journal*, page 9.

Tadadjeu, M. (2004). African Language Needs in Information and Communication Technology (ICT). page 9.

Tunde, O. (2012). Investigating the Language Situation in Africa. In *Language and Law*, Language rights, pages 272–293. Oxford Handbooks in Linguistics, Great Clarendon street.

Vydrin, V., Rovenchak, A., and Maslinsky, K. (2016). Maninka Reference Corpus: A Presentation. In *TALAf 2016 : Traitement automatique des langues africaines (écrit et parole). Atelier JEP-TALN-RECITAL 2016 - Paris le*, Paris, France, July.

9. Language Resource References

De Pauw, Guy and Waiganjo Wagacha, Peter and de Schryver, Gilles-Maurice. (2009). *The SAWA corpus: a parallel corpus English - Swahili*.

Mboning, Elvis and NTeALan contributors. (2017). *NTeALan lexicographic African language resources: an open-source REST API*. NTeALan Project, distributed via NTeALan, Bantu resources, 1.0.

Vydrin, Valentin and Rovenchak, Andrij and Maslinsky, Kirill. (2016). *Maninka Reference Corpus: A Presentation*. Speecon Project, distributed via ELRA, Madingue resources, 1.0, ISLRN 613-489-674-355-0.